the WISDOM of WOMEN

Models for Faith and Action

**Bishops' Committee on Women
in Society and in the Church**
National Conference of Catholic Bishops

In its 1991 planning document, as approved by the general membership of the National Conference of Catholic Bishops in November 1990, the Bishops' Committee on Women in Society and in the Church was authorized to prepare a pastoral resource based on the 1990 national Wisdom of Women Symposium. This publication, designed to share what took place at the symposium with a wider audience, is that resource. The text has been approved by the members of the NCCB Committee on Women in Society and in the Church and is authorized for publication by the undersigned.

May 16, 1991

Monsignor Robert N. Lynch
General Secretary
NCCB/USCC

ISBN 1-55586-430-9

"The Will of God," by Jessica Powers, Sister of Miriam of the Holy Spirit, in *Selected Poetry of Jessica Powers*, copyright © 1989 by Sheed & Ward, Kansas City, Missouri. Used with permission. All rights reserved.

The Measure of My Days by Florida Scott-Maxwell © 1968 Florida Scott-Maxwell. Reprinted by permission of Alfred A. Knopf.

Excerpts from "Litany for Survival," by Audre Lorde, as found in *Talking Back: Thinking Feminist; Thinking Black*, by Belle Hooks (Boston: South End Press) copyright © 1989 by Audre Lorde. Excerpts from "The City of Freedom" as found in *Sister Outsider: Essays and Speeches* (The Crossing Press) copyright © 1984 by Audre Lorde. All rights reserved. Every effort has been made to obtain reprint permission for these excerpts.

Copyright © 1991 by the United States Catholic Conference, Inc.; Washington, D.C. All rights reserved. No part of this work may be reproduced or transmitted in any form or by any means, electronic or mechanical, including photocopying, recording, or by any information storage and retrieval system, without permission in writing from the copyright owner.

Acknowledgments

Thanks are due to many people who cooperated in making The Wisdom of Women Symposium the success it was, many more than I can name here.

A steering committee worked with me for over a year preparing the symposium: Maria Guarracino of the Archdiocese of New York; Annette Kane, executive director of the National Council of Catholic Women; Winkie Le Fils, U.S. representative to the World Union of Catholic Women's Organizations; Sally Malhoit of the Diocese of Toledo; and Phyllis Willerscheidt of the Archdiocese of St. Paul-Minneapolis. All helped to shape the symposium; their leadership was indispensable.

Sheila Garcia, staff assistant in the Secretariat for Laity and Family Life, was tireless in her efforts to organize The Wisdom of Women Symposium. The bishops who serve on the NCCB Committee on Women in Society and in the Church took an active role at all stages and in many ways. Katharine Bird, who worked as writer and general editor in assembling this book, has been exceptionally patient and careful throughout the project.

My deepest appreciation to all.

Dolores Leckey
Executive Director
Secretariat for Laity and Family Life
National Conference of Catholic Bishops

Contents

I. **Introduction / 1**

II. **Model Keynote Addresses / 5**

　On Conversion and Listening to Women
　　Bishop Matthew Clark / 7

　Women's Contributions to Culture
　　Sidney Callahan / 17

　One Tapestry: Many Voices, Many Colors
　　Diana Hayes / 28

　Reflection Questions / 31

III. **Model Panel Discussions / 33**

　Forum on Women in the Diocesan Church / 35
　　Reflection Questions / 42

　Collaborative Ministry / 43
　　Reflection Questions / 49

　Open Forum / 50
　　Reflection Questions / 54

IV. **Workshops in Action / 55**

　Women in Canon Law
　　Sister Sharon Euart, RSM / 57
　　Reflection Questions / 67

Pro-Life and Feminist?
    Helen Alvaré / 68
        Reflection Questions / 70
What Is Women's Unique Spirituality?
    Dana Greene / 71
        Reflection Questions / 73
Women and Aging: An Outline / 74
Other Topics for Workshop Development / 77

V. Spiritual Exercises / 79

Morning Prayer Service
    Prepared by the Diocese of Saginaw / 80
Concluding Prayer Service
    Prepared by the National Council of
    Catholic Women / 82

VI. Wrap-Up / 85

Framing a Call to Action
    Susan Muto / 87
A Vision for the Future
    Bishop Joseph Imesch / 92
Voices of Women / 94
Reflection Questions / 98

VII. Resources / 99

Sample Outline for Two-Day Workshop / 100
Sample Outline for One-Day Workshop / 102
Sample Outline for Four-Part
Adult Education Series / 104
Membership Roster, Bishops' Committee on
Women in Society and in the Church (1989-1992) / 107
Selected Bibliography / 108
Additional Resources / 110

Introduction

The Wisdom of Women: Models for Faith and Action grew out of the November 1990 symposium, sponsored by the U.S. Bishops' Committee on Women in Society and in the Church. The invitation-only symposium, which was held in Washington, D.C., attracted 200 women chosen by their bishops to attend because of their commitment to women's issues and their dedication to and love for the Catholic Church. A number of men, among them bishops from the committee, also attended.

This resource is designed for use on the parish and diocesan levels by individuals, groups, and organizations who wish to implement and stimulate discussion on the contributions and concerns of women today in society and in the Church. The dialogue and questions raised at the symposium addressed many vital issues that are of concern to people throughout all levels of the Church and society, and this resource provides a way of sharing some of that with a much wider audience.

The book includes the following components:

- brief introductions, explaining what is included in each of the major sections;

- excerpts from the symposium's plenary sessions;

- model workshops that can be used intact or adapted to local situations and needs;

- a sample panel discussion that illustrates how women's commissions address interests of pressing concern to women on the diocesan level;
- a sample panel on collaborative ministry that illustrates various aspects of this type of ministry;
- "voices" of women that appear throughout the book, both in questions presented to the two panels and in a separate open-forum session in the Wrap-Up section (These "voices" comprise a rich tapestry, representing the diversity of women in the Catholic Church in the United States.);
- reflection questions at the end of most sections (These are intended to initiate a discussion of the issues at your local level.); and
- a resource section that includes model outlines for a one-day and a two-day workshop; a sample outline for a four-part adult education series; a current membership roster of the Bishops' Committee on Women in Society and in the Church (1989-1992); and a selected bibliography.

We encourage you to use this book to facilitate continuing discussion on women in your local area. It can be used by a wide variety of groups in various ways, for example:

- parish study groups or parish "town meetings";
- women's groups;
- parish pastoral councils;
- in-service days for priests and educators;
- diocesan groups, including diocesan pastoral councils or convocations of lay groups; and
- parent and alumni groups of various institutions of education.

Please regard this book as a working model, to be adapted as needed to meet your special circumstances. The materials provided here can be used to stimulate discussion or to provide background material as you study women's contributions and concerns, both in society and in the Church.

Our November symposium lasted several days, but depending on local circumstances, a shorter period of time works well too. A one-day workshop can focus on a few issues in depth; a longer period of time works admirably when discussing several issues. An evening or an afternoon seminar can zoom in tightly on one burning issue.

However long or brief your workshop or seminar may be, always remember to include the spiritual elements. We found our prayer sessions and eucharistic celebrations to be among the most moving and most powerful parts of the symposium. Praying together put us in a suitable frame of mind to listen attentively and respectfully to each other—especially when we did not agree totally on an issue.

We hope you find this a helpful resource. Please let us know how you use it and how well it served to stimulate your discussions regarding the contributions and concerns of women in society and in the Church.

Dolores Leckey
Executive Director
Secretariat for Laity and Family Life
National Conference of Catholic Bishops

Model Keynote Addresses

How you begin a symposium, conference, or workshop on women is vital to its success. The first step is to choose a keynote speaker who has expertise in the area you are addressing and, preferably, a dynamic speaking style. An outstanding keynote speaker inspires and stimulates listeners by:

- clarifying the areas the issue covers;

- sharing personal experiences relating to the issue; and

- offering suggestions as to how and where the issue might be addressed during the symposium as well as in the days, months, and years to come.

In sum, the keynote speaker covers the past, the present, and the future in a speech that should leave listeners ready and eager to discuss the issue from their own experience.

Three Models

Part II presents three different keynote models for use in a discussion of women and their concerns. Excerpts of two addresses and a reflection given during The Wisdom of Women Symposium are presented here by way of example only; they are to impart an essence of the symposium and offer guidance as you develop your own workshop or conference.

The three speakers discussed conversion, each in a strikingly unique way, building on his or her own experience of the journey toward understanding women and their issues today.

The Speakers

Bishop Matthew Clark, of the Diocese of Rochester, New York, was elected chairman of the Bishops' Committee on Women in Society and in the Church in 1989. During his twelve years as bishop of Rochester, he has supported women in their efforts to help the Church to understand better the needs and concerns of women in the Church and in society. Bishop Clark's keynote, which opened The Wisdom of Women Symposium, tells of his long road to *conversion* on the issue of women.

Sidney Callahan, whose early career paralleled that of many Catholic women of the 1950s who became wives and mothers, is a professor of psychology at Mercy College, Dobbs Ferry, New York. She points out that her 1955 college degree and her 1980 doctorate in psychology were earned on the twenty-five-year plan. Dr. Callahan is the author of numerous articles and books, including *With All Our Heart and Mind: The Spiritual Works of Mercy in a Psychological Age* (Crossroads-Continuum, 1988). Dr. Callahan's address approaches *conversion* from a psychological perspective, namely, from an understanding of how gender has interacted with culture in the United States over the years.

Diana Hayes is a professor of theology at Georgetown University in Washington, D.C. She is a member of the Washington Resource Group, whose members provide assistance to the Bishops' Committee on Women as needed. Dr. Hayes says she speaks as a woman of color to remind us how important it is to include women of color in any discussion of women and their concerns. *Conversion* from her perspective includes the discovery that we all stand to discover much as we listen to and learn from each other.

Model 1
On Conversion and Listening to Women
Bishop Matthew Clark

I am honored to be the keynote speaker for this symposium. [Preparing for the address] has forced me to review experiences that have been deeply significant in my continuing development as a human being and in my ongoing formation as a bishop in the Church.

I wish also to speak of the future and the dreams that we hold in common about making our Church and our world communities in which all can more fully enjoy the freedom, the life-giving relationships, the hopes, the rich justice, and profound peace for which God made us.

Conversion

At its root, the word [*conversion*] means to turn, to turn again, or to return. Webster [defines] conversion as: "a physical transformation from one state or form to another; a change in character, form or function; a spiritual change from sinfulness to righteousness."

The *Westminster Dictionary of Christian Theology* recognizes the traditional religious meanings of the word: a turn from idols to the living God; the call of God in Christ; change in affiliation; change from noninvolvement to affiliation. Then it notes a change that has occurred in theological thinking. That shift is away from an understanding of conversion as merely the initial turning to faith or to a religious group and toward an understanding of conversion as the transformation of the whole individual over an entire lifetime.

Such a lifelong process of transformation occurs through a combination of intellectual activity, emotional maturation, increasing ethical vigor and sensitivity, and intensifying of the religious love of God and humanity. Such a notion of conversion certainly includes the recognition of a need occasionally, even daily, to turn away from sin in the specific moral sense of that term. But it includes much more than that.

As I understand this notion of conversion, it recognizes such human realities as the achievement of new insight, changing perspectives, and fresh possibilities. It enables discrimination between essentials and accidentals and positively encourages the reimagining of daily reality in such a way as to allow us to break through human constructs that limit freedoms and dampen the spirit.

Conversion in this sense opens paths to new experience, creates opportunities to reflect on it and share it with others, and allows us to come to fresh personal and communal moments of reintegration. It is a process that helps us to understand and to learn from what has gone before. It also helps us to engage in the exciting creative task of shaping the future.

Such an understanding of conversion is much in keeping with the Church's self-awareness and self-expression in Vatican Council II. Conciliar expressions such as "a pilgrim people" and "a Church always in need of reform" carry with them both the notion of continuity and the notion of change.

To be on pilgrimage implies that completion is not yet present. We are not yet at home. And, although we know that what God has begun in us will one day be brought to completion, we are also aware both of our tendency to sin and of the reality and effects of our sin. It is for that reason the Church recognizes its need for ongoing reform—to move away from sin, of course, but to move to structures, dispositions, and practices that expand people's creative capacities, spark their hopes, and stand in support of their God-given freedoms.

Conversion as I understand it and speak of it here is a dynamic, lifelong, experience-based, spirit-sparked process by which persons and communities perceive more clearly the inner truth of God's love, as that love is revealed in Christ through the power of the Holy Spirit, and respond to that love with a deeper consistency and integrity.

In my judgment, it is one of the prime means we have at our disposal to deal with the tension that comes with the need at once to maintain continuity and to change. To accept the realities of the pilgrimage and our need for ongoing conversion is to be freed truly to deal with the dynamic nature of our tradition of faith. That has always meant holding as precious and preserving all that God has revealed to us in Christ through the power of the Holy Spirit.

But such holding and preserving do not freeze us nor should they ever leave us yearning to restore the Church's life and practice to that of some former age. Rather, the life and love revealed and shared with us in Christ impel successive generations of Christians always to search for deeper life, sharper insight, more loving relationships, and the grace to live and proclaim the Gospel to all.

Personal Experiences of Conversion

In the eleven and one-half years I have had the privilege of serving as the bishop of Rochester [New York], I think I have experienced the kind of conversion I have just tried to describe. I believe that this conversion has included more than my perception of and commitment to the dignity and place of women in the Church. But that issue is at the core of my own growth, and the women of our diocese have been the prime catalysts in that growth. Let me explain that as simply and directly as I can.

My Years in Rome

I have spent a good deal of my adult life in the city of Rome. Of the twenty years between 1959, the beginning of my theological studies, and 1979, the year of my ordination as a bishop, I spent thirteen of those years in Rome. Those years are rich in memory for me, and they are so, I think, because of the conversion and growth that occurred in me and my companions in that wonderful place.

I was in Rome for three of the four sessions of Vatican Council II. Life was exciting then; people we now regard as heroes—like John Courtney Murray—were all over the town, joining in the search, pooling their wisdom, seeking to advance the renewal of the Church and a more fruitful dialogue between the Church and the world.

Rome is the "City of Popes," and I think this evening of the four remarkable men who have held the chair of Peter during my years there. I remember the warmth, the courage, the incredible seminal vision of John XXIII. I grow in respect each day for Paul VI, whose charge it was to cultivate the seed John planted and who did so with such balance and humaneness. Often I wonder what would the Church be like today if the ministry of John Paul I as bishop of Rome had lasted longer than thirty-three days. And daily, I stand in union with John Paul II, by whose hands I was ordained a bishop and with whom I and the other bishops share in pastoral care for all of the churches.

I mention those four wonderful pilgrims because in each of them I find some particular expression of the richness of the Church at Rome.

My new ministry in Rome [invited] me to go a bit deeper into my vocation as priest. My last assignment in my home diocese of Albany had been as director of the newly formed priests' personnel board. Those years 1969 to 1972 [were] a time of much excitement, uncertainty, and some real searching.

Many of our brother priests were leaving during those years—I think about twenty during my brief term on the personnel board. We were still spinning from the controversy surrounding the issuance of *Humanae Vitae*. Liturgical reform, ecumenical initiatives, and a fresh sense of engagement with the culture in which the Church is incarnate were exciting ventures that inspired many of us, but they were also the occasion for some discord and pain—even among people like ourselves.

Rome for me was a privileged place to be just at that moment. The call to a new ministry was truly a call to conversion. It was not a conversion one describes in terms of *good* and *evil* so much as in terms of *awareness, clarity, conviction,* and *integration*. I know that I had places to go in my commitment to prayer, in reflection, and in integration of the experiences I had up to that time.

People Who Helped Along the Way

In God's gracious providence, I found those years to be filled with gifts of discovery and deepening. There were several human sources most responsible for those good gifts. One was a patient, gifted Jesuit spiritual director, who helped me to mature in my understanding of and approach to prayer. Another, also a Jesuit, was a psychologist at the Gregorian University's Institute of Psychology, whose expert assistance allowed me to come to some freeing, life-giving discoveries about myself, which I would have taken years to come to on my own.

The opportunity to be in the Church of Rome broadened my sense of the Church. One can not be in Rome very long without being made deeply aware that the sun never sets on Catholic life. And inseparably a part of that experience is the realization that the Church's makeup is truly catholic with a small "c."

In recent years, most especially during the pastoral service of John Paul II, another aspect of Rome's ministry has been highlighted: her care for all of the churches and her special call to confirm the faith of her sisters and brothers and to promote unity among us all.

My own episcopal ordination at the hands of John Paul II in the company of twenty-five other candidates from eleven countries on five continents will always remain a rich memory, in which I can appreciate that we are a communion of faith, that to "go it alone" is foreign to Catholic life, that we are a community rich in diversity yet called to that kind of unity in faith and charity that allows us credibly to proclaim the Good News of salvation.

My Years in Rochester

On June 26, 1979, I was installed as the eighth bishop of Rochester. Some of you were there that evening. It was a splendid evening in every way, and although I was in a state bordering on total shock, I enjoyed the warmth and hospitality of the people who formed that local Church.

But even in the glow of that marvelous June evening, there were intimations that the past was indeed prelude and that I would be called to ongoing conversions through the people, events, and circumstances of my new ministry. On that June evening as we gathered for the celebration, a group of women wearing yellow sashes were distributing leaflets to all who would accept them. They were members of the Women's Ordination Conference, which at that time had its national headquarters in that city.

In my early days in Rochester, I discovered that while not all agreed with all of the goals of the Women's Ordination Conference, a great number of people were very much in sympathy with any initiative that would open minds and hearts to new possibilities for women in our Church. And I soon learned that my own mind and heart would be tested to see what my dispositions were about that lively and sensitive issue. . . .

I do not mean that my reception by the people was in any way hostile. Much to the contrary. I have always been treated with kindness and care by the wonderful people of our diocese. But I would be less than honest if I said that they did not challenge me and challenge me quite strongly about the themes that bring us together.

In the customary round of get-acquainted meetings, questions were raised again and again: What do you think about women in the Church? . . . about women preaching? . . . about young girls serving at the altar? . . . about the ordination of women?

Fundamental Insights on Women

I remember trying to be open to new ideas. In the experience of meeting the women and men of Rochester I came to two fundamental insights. First, that the bishop must learn from his people before he can be a good teacher or servant.

The Rome that I loved then and still do is a highly clerical place, where women are not very visible and do not have significant influence. I began to realize that my lack of pastoral interaction with women during the years I spent overseas had left me in a deficit position in our local Church. The people among whom I was asked to stand in a position of pastoral leadership, I was learning, had much to teach me in this regard. I knew that I had to open myself to their experience, or I could never hope to be a credible leader among them.

To do that I needed to develop a perspective, a vision, a pastoral disposition that honored the best traditions of our Church, that would be forged through collaboration between myself and the community, and to which all of us could commit ourselves and move forward. A group of thirty-plus persons, four-fifths of them women, and I met for a series of meetings during which we tried to do just that. I committed myself at least for the first Saturday morning meeting—and I think for a second—to do absolutely nothing but listen. Though the experience was painful at times, it is among the best things I have ever done.

By that time, I knew many of the participants very well. I knew them as highly intelligent, totally loyal, generous, prayerful members of our faith community. When they told me of their experience as women in the Church and of the pain that was attached to so much of that experience, it had a deep effect on me. They shared with me the truth they held in their hearts. I knew it was a truth that I had to take very seriously.

The upshot of that experience was the publication, on April 29, 1982, the feast of Catherine of Siena, of *The Fire in the Thornbush*, a pastoral letter on women later published by *Origins* under the title, "American Catholic Women: Persistent Questions, Faithful Witness." It bears my name as author, and I did give much to it; but it truly is a letter that was born from the wisdom of the community, and it was a further step in my own ongoing conversion.

The second strong insight I wanted to mention was that our local Churches, our dioceses, have distinct histories and diverse ethnic compositions; are different in size and populations; have varied resources, limitations, and dreams.

Surely, we profess one faith and, surely, we belong to a visible communion, the center of which is the Church of Rome. But we are different indeed. It would be fun to exemplify that by inviting the representatives here from the dioceses of Pensacola-Tallahassee, Seattle, and New York City to come forward and to compare notes about what your local Churches are like, how things get done, what your resources are, what problems you are facing, what is most promising locally, and what is of greatest concern. My guess is that we would discover a profound commonality in faith and other values but an incredible range of differences in the responses to those particular questions.

Hopes for the Future

In conclusion, I want to express some hopes I have for the Church as we move toward the year 2000. My experience of ministry in our local Church has shaped these ideas. The women of our Church have been much a part of that shaping. I expect that they will play an even greater part in our ongoing conversion.

I hope for a continuing renewal and reestablishment of our rich Catholic tradition of the local Church.

My hope [is] that the local Churches will continually become freer than they presently are to make the significant pastoral judgments by which they shape the concrete ways in which they celebrate and proclaim the faith. The more particular the matter, the more freedom should the local Churches enjoy.

I hope that we will find more satisfactory ways to honor and be enriched by the wisdom of the people of God, especially as that wisdom is born of and relates to their daily experience of the faith.

The people are to be full, active participants in the life of the Church. This implies that they, holy and gifted in the Spirit, have wisdom as well as service to share with all for the common good. This kind of association and interaction with the people has deep implications. It requires that the one who would teach must be willing continually to learn. It recognizes the lived experience of the faith community as a source for theological reflection and, therefore, as an ongoing source of conversion for all in the community.

I hope that we as a Church will become more expansive and inclusive in our ways of thinking and acting and will be unafraid to explore fully and courageously the questions that are active in the hearts of so many of the people of God.

The Church is most alive when she is expansive and inclusive, when she stands in dialogue with the time and culture in which she is enfleshed, when she searches for truth wherever it may be found, when she expresses fully the truth she bears in language that speaks to the people of the age. At her best, the Church finds room for all manner of diversity, disallowing only those points of view or directions that deny the central mysteries of our faith. Consequently, she will be slow to draw lines defining the spiritual condition of her members or to exclude people from her communion. She will be more inclined to speak of "both/and," rather than "either/or." Nor will she decide complex issues before she has heard all appropriate voices in the community or before the issue at hand has come to maturity or, even if it has, before there is a compelling need to settle the matter.

> *I hope that the Church, under the leadership of whoever is successor to Peter and at his request, will be willing fully and carefully to hear the wisdom of the people as they express their convictions about some of the issues that cause tensions in the Church today.*

Permit me to mention five of them:

> **Birth Control.** According to all evidence I have read and based on my experience, it seems that the practice of large numbers of Catholic people in the area of regulation of birth is not in accord with the official teaching of the Church. In my opinion, that is unfortunate for all of us, because it tends to separate bishops from the people and to weaken the teaching authority of the Church. Most important, I am afraid that the gulf that apparently exists between the official teaching of the Church and the reception of this teaching by the faithful depresses our capacity to address credibly other topics in the area of sexuality. People say more often than I would like to hear: "You do not understand sexuality in marriage" or "We cannot possibly live up to that." Further, many persons simply disengage from any conversation with us.

> **Abortion.** Another issue that invites our careful listening involves the question of abortion, which is so troublesome and divisive in our nation. This issue will challenge our pastoral sensitivity for years to come. My particular hope is that we will do a better job than we have done in hearing the women and men of our Church on this issue. We will only be helped in our pastoral practice by hearing those who conceive and those who bear new life in their womb and who, for whatever reason, struggle with the question of whether or not they will carry that new life to full term.

Celibacy. The requirement of a commitment to lifelong celibacy in those who wish to be ordained priests in the Latin Church is yet another issue where the Church needs to be open to hearing the concerns and questions of her people. Many people are concerned—and so am I—that this requirement is a human construct that stands in the way of the Church's eucharistic life. In my judgment, there exist so many questions around this discipline and around its relationship to the priesthood, and therefore to the Eucharist, that the Church would be well served by a careful, full reconsideration and weighing of the advantages and disadvantages of this practice.

Ordination of Women. The question of the suitability of women for ordination to the ministerial priesthood is also an issue that invites our willing attentiveness. This issue is without question a lively one among very large numbers of Roman Catholics. That reality has been verified by all of the studies and surveys that I have read or about which I have heard. It has most certainly been a part of my experience within our local Church and in other local Churches in our country that I have visited. It was most emphatically commented on in the reflections—written and oral—that people offered to our writing committee when we were preparing the draft of our pastoral letter, *Partners in the Mystery of Redemption*. To declare a matter closed does not close the matter nor does it stop the questioning of the faithful.

Election of Bishops. I hope that there will be steps taken to establish a process for the selection of bishops that will provide for a clear, public, and significant contribution by the local Church in which the person named will be serving. We have experienced a variety of ways of selecting bishops in the history of our Church: from acclamation to our present system, which is not highly participatory. I am not exactly sure how episcopal selection might best be done, but I think it would be good for the health of the Church were we to reform this process, which is of such significance for the local Churches. The wisdom of the people is rich, and we are enriched when we enjoy it in as full a manner as possible.

Conclusion

I am very much aware that there are other hopes I hold for the Church of tomorrow and for next year—indeed, for the year 2000—which I have not mentioned. For example, I have not spoken of the Church's call to concern herself with, to learn from, and to identify herself with the poor. Nor have I treated explicitly the ecumenical enterprise in which we need to be consistently and eagerly engaged. But I do hold those near to my heart and commit myself to them as critical aspects of our ecclesial life.

I have selected the issues outlined in this talk because I think that they relate to our capacity more credibly and fruitfully to proclaim the gospel in today's culture, at least in the culture of the United States. Insofar as we appear to be unable or unwilling to wrestle with the real questions that are alive in both the minds and hearts of faithful people, our capacity both to nourish their faith and to proclaim the gospel to others is diminished.

I know we will never be totally who we would like to be until Christ's work in us is complete. The Church is not simply in need of reform. It is always in need of reform. Or to use another image: We are a pilgrim people whose journey is by the light of faith, who need always to be ready to follow the lead of the Holy Spirit and, if need be, to leave safe and familiar places when God calls us to new places.

If this sort of journeying tends to discourage us, we need to remember that Jesus promised to be with us always, and Jesus Christ is always faithful.

Model 2
Women's Contributions to Culture
Sidney Callahan

Women have contributed to culture in the past, do so in the present, and will continue to do so in the future. It is far easier to analyze the present role of women than it is to penetrate the reality of the past, but the past is always worth examination and reflection. We need to know where we have come from in order to know where we should go. As the feminine artist Judy Chicago said, "Our heritage is our power."

Within the historical era in Western culture, men have been dominant and in charge of recorded history. Men and the educated elite of males have used education and literacy to describe and codify the culture, to define who is who and what is what. So a subordinate, uneducated group such as the majority of women could only be reduced to silence.

Women and women's nature were for the most part defined and evaluated by men. Even when outstanding women were educated and rose to cultural prominence, they stood a good chance of soon being overlooked and quickly forgotten. Until recent centuries only queens, great female saints, and Mary, the Mother of God, were exceptions to the general rule of female obscurity.

Today, with the resurgence of feminism and the appearance of many women scholars, women's contributions to culture in the past have begun to be rediscovered and recovered. Women's hidden history is slowly being revealed, both the achievements as well as the painful distracting history of cultural suppression, denigration, wasted talents, and trivializations. Sometimes it is very painful to read about the past of women, and I think we have to do it just so we will know.

Subtle and not so subtle discrimination still goes on today in many parts of our society. To show you what it is like to be silenced or to be forgotten, I will remind you of an experience that many of you, probably with your own eyes and ears, have also had.

In a working group of men with a minority of women—maybe one woman—a woman will put forth a suggestion that is more or less ignored by the majority of males present. Several minutes later, a high status male makes the same point and gets instant response and applause for his contribution.

Women still can be invisible in a public, male-dominated world. There is something about being invisible and totally not listened to that begins to make you doubt whether one has anything to say or not, or whether one even did say anything.

If this has always been true, sort of a little parable of the historical process, how can we learn about the past contributions of women to culture? Well, happily, new waves of scholars are reexamining the past with a new eye—not new tools—that goes beyond standard accounts and the official story. For example: [A friend] told me about a wonderful book where a man had reexamined midwife accounts in Holland in, I think, the fourteenth or fifteenth century. It is very interesting that he seems to have found that women were not totally callous to the deaths of their children. Male historians have said that people really did not value children and [yet the midwife accounts reveal] interesting questions about what to do when people go into decline and depression over miscarriage and so forth. But until you start reading midwife accounts you do not really learn about a lot of the things that may be going on in a certain era.

Looking at the Past with New Eyes

There are doubt and suspicion of the culturally sanctioned versions of events. Since the victor always gets to write up the accounts of the battle, and a power elite baptizes the status quo, a scholar has to dig and use detective work to find out what really happened in the past.

Many social historians, not just women and feminists, are now interested in the lives of ordinary persons in their daily living. They are doing what is known as "bottom up" history, and since women have always been at the bottom, "bottom up" history has a lot to do with women's lives.

What kind of new accounts of women's lives and works have come to the fore in this new scholarship? A few themes have surfaced repeatedly and may be included in future textbooks, although you can never be sure.

Old and New Testament Images

In the Old Testament, scholars are reclaiming and reinterpreting many original texts that were once interpreted as misogynist. God as Mother as well as Father is reappearing in material images. Certainly, the female figure of Wisdom, or Wisdom Woman in the Old Testament, has been fruitfully reexamined.

Feminist scholarship has also reinterpreted early Christian communities as having women functioning as equals and in leadership roles in the early house churches.

It is also all too clear that as the centuries passed, the revolutionary gospel of equality given to women was suppressed. It is quite easy to follow that process. Today, the Church and theological scholarship are finally and fully reclaiming women's equal Christian dignity.

Great Women of the Past

At the same time, many of the great women of the Church who had been almost forgotten are being rediscovered. I, for instance, have had two discoveries in the last few years. I have only recently heard of the great Hildegard of Bingen, the influential scholarly abbess, nor had I ever heard of the Beguines, the lay order of women in Holland who were suppressed.

The iron law of cultural amnesia operates. First to discredit, then to suppress, and finally to forget. Lifting the repression and recovering the past will then take considerable effort.

Female Helpmates

Another line of feminist religion as inquiry and recovering of women's cultural influence centers on rediscovering the unheralded relationships of great men to their female helpmates. Again and again it appears that the wife of the genius, or the sister of the author, or the daughter of the artist was a silent collaborator in the work. The mother, wife, sister, daughter, or mistress could never be publicly acknowledged and so their accomplishments have been almost lost to history.

Women Writers

We can now understand why so many women writers in the nineteenth century, such as George Sand, George Eliot, or the Brontë sisters, felt a need to begin their publishing careers using male names.

Writing has always attracted women because it can be done at home and then sent to critics who may not know which gender produced the work. Women writers do not have to get into the face-to-face struggles that disadvantage women in other careers and in other forms of public life.

Drawing from the Wisdom of Women. Bishop Matthew Clark, bishop of Rochester, New York, and chairman of the NCCB Committee on Women in Society and in the Church, listens intently during the symposium's plenary session. To his right is Annette Kane, executive director of the National Council of Catholic Women.

For this reason, in the past, women have influenced public culture more through their writing then in any other way. The writers outnumber amazing women reformers like Florence Nightingale or Dorothy Day. Maybe Harriet Beecher Stowe did not start the Civil War all by herself—as intimated by Lincoln when he said, "Oh, is this the little lady who started the Civil War?"—when she wrote *Uncle Tom's Cabin*, but she did influence America's cultural repudiation of slavery.

Women in the Home

No one should ever underestimate the cultural power of stories, imagery, and art. Women who write, read, and tell stories to the young are creating the future of a culture. In fact, this traditional familial socializing role of women is still a potent and perennial contribution to culture.

The traditional Western gender role of women has been a culturally creative one, and it both constituted and transmitted culture in the family. My mother came today to visit me here, and I was telling her about this conference and what I was going to say. I was saying, "It is all about women and culture," and she said, "Women and culture? Women *are* culture."

The Feminine Role in Western Culture

I would like to describe the riches of this traditional role and then discuss how I think modern mainstream feminism has built upon women's strengths in creating a public vision of women's equality in the culture.

The idea of the feminine role in Western culture has waxed and waned, but generally I think it had more strengths then weaknesses. I see this traditional feminine ideal as one of nurturance and care. Think of the great Marian prayers asking for mercy, comfort, sweetness, life, and hope as from a mother to a child. Instead of the power and logic of domination in conflict, which has been a masculine ideal, women have embraced the power of actualization engendered through nurturing love.

Women have again and again in history been drawn to ideals of creative nurturance expressed in many different activities. Women have been biologically fruitful and materially creative in their childbearing and childrearing. Women have been nurturing in actualizing and preserving their family ties, their friendships, and their religious and secular communities dedicated to wisdom.

What today makes most women different from men? If you were a Martian arriving on this earth, what would be your estimate as you looked around? Well, women give birth to you; they feed and clothe you; they sustain your family customs and kinship ties. Women are practical, resourceful, wise, believers, and best of all, women, unlike most modern men, have friends. Men have wives, but women have to have friends.

Is this too romantic a view of the traditional feminine virtues, a sort of simple-minded replay of the cult of ideal womanhood? I do not think so, especially if we realistically put into the picture and balance it with assessment of negative tendencies.

Yes, there is an underside to the traditional feminine role, and these dangers have been well recognized as *passivity, inertia, dissipation, self-destructive denial,* and *manipulation.* Admittedly, powerlessness can corrupt as much as power. But women as a group still today seem to have many advantages.

Women's Way of Relating

In U.S. culture, there are still some things that psychologists see as different: females talk earlier, are more cooperative and animated in their play and friendships, and use more cooperative and enabling speech patterns than do males. We have no idea how important these are for conversation and working together.

Women are known for using kinds of speech that allow you to talk; for asking you questions: "Do you think this is the way we ought to do it?"; for putting tag-ends on questions: "Is it?"; instead of "This is the way we ought to do it," which is a more assertive style that closes the conversation. This is something that seems to be built into little girls and little boys very early in their play styles. Some of the most astute psychologists do not think that this comes from the family but, rather, is something that happens in the peer group.

Women are less violently aggressive and self-destructive than men. Women possess more moral values and display more empathy and sympathy. Women are more religious and engage in more charitable volunteer activity. If one can indulge in female chauvinism for a minute, one could reverse Henry Higgins' cries in "My Fair Lady" and say: "Why can't a man be more like a women. All in all, we're a marvelous sex."

It is also a cultural reality that, from childhood on, women are often dominated and intimidated by males, who are more physically aggressive and competitive. Psychologists suggest that is why boys and girls choose to play in different groups. Girls, because they have more intimate friendships and cooperative styles, feel they can influence each other. Little girls cannot influence boys; boys are more aggressive. According to one psychologist, "Men seem to need the group structure in their kind of rough and tumble play, and girls are intimidated and often get pushed around. They are aggressive and assertive too, but with boys, they tend to be dominated."

Women have been drawn to conflict resolution and strategies of peace partly out of necessity. In raising children and in keeping households going, women have had to become experts in cooperation, in getting intractable males and difficult children to move toward neutral goals. Women have to be shrewd in overcoming inner and outer obstacles so that the family can go on. We do not call human intelligence "mother wit" for nothing. These nurturing skills of cooperating and resourceful managing can be as valuable in public as in private life.

The traditional feminine gender role has been a handicap when entering our public political culture. Women and women's ways have been labeled as *weak, unreliable,* and *irrational,* while at the same time women have been exploited by men and the power elite. Women have not been and still are not appreciated.

Women's Volunteer Nurturing

Women's work in the family, in the Church, and in other cultural groups lacks status, basically, I think, because it is volunteer work. Unpaid domestic work is the mainstay of every family, and almost all women who work outside the home also work at what has been called the "second shift" when they come home.

And who generally takes care of elderly parents and other relatives in need of assistance? Women's volunteer labor sustains their communities. Without the women of my town, the churches, the political parties, the PTA, the League of Women Voters, the Scouts, the hospitals, the environmental groups, and numerous charities would all grind to a halt. Women are the unpaid caretakers of the world.

I do not think that women resent their nurturing and free service, because there is no freer act than doing things out of love and commitment for no monetary gain. Besides, to give is to get; to love is to be loved. But women do not want to be penalized culturally for their loving nurturance.

Why don't women who work at home receive social security credit? Why aren't women who do the work in the community recognized as important? Why are we such an anti-child society, with so little public support for family life, or for divorced and abandoned women? Women are creating our civilization's future by their caretaking of children in their community. Yet, in a culture that glorifies success in the marketplace or the jungle mentality of survival of the fittest, women's work does not count. Actualizing nurturing power is overlooked, and rewards go to those with power to control, to dominate many subordinates, and to produce tangible technological services. Women—and all others in the Church and in society—have to rebel against this destructive value structure, which permeates our society and is perpetuated largely by the media.

Feminism as a Force for Good

The mainstream feminists' movement, in my opinion, has been a force for women's liberation and the renewal of our culture. While modern feminists come in all varieties, the roots of mainstream feminism are solidly within the Christian good news of equality: All human beings are made in the image of God. Jesus treated women in a revolutionary way. Scripture tells us that, in Christ, all are unified in the kingdom. In the kingdom, the Spirit blows where it lists [desires] and the ways of the world are turned inside out. I love that phrase, the idea that the Church should be the world turned inside out. This was radical good news for women, who were often exploited for their domestic labor and sexual and reproductive utility.

Although the American roots of feminism in the nineteenth century were even more overtly Christian in inspiration, modern mainstream feminism has crystallized much of the Christian message of equality of persons. One good effect of feminism and feminists' consciousness raising has been to bring the Christian values of love, justice, nurturance, and equality of persons into our political discourse in a new way.

Women as Peacemakers

The raising of feminine consciousness in the culture has also helped the peace movement. Women hate violence and aggression since they are often victims of the same. They know what it is to be defined as different and thereby to be a target. Women have also resisted raising their sons to become cannon fodder. Maternal care and loving investment in each young body ensure that women can never look at casualty lists unmoved. It is not an accident that some of the most influential passivists in American life have been women. We can take pride in our own Dorothy Day.

Women have also been advocates for equal justice and influential in human rights movements: the women of the Black Sash, protesting apartheid in South Africa, share a commonality with the women in South America, struggling against state torture and murder, and with the women in our own South, dealing with racism and its legacy.

Women and the Pro-Life Movement

Women have been marginal citizens and know what it is to be deemed a nonperson. They can take up the cause of those who are thought to be expendable. Women, for instance, are the grass-roots workers in the pro-life movement and in the pregnancy crisis centers dedicated to serving women and their unborn children. I work at one of these pregnancy counseling centers. All the people who staff the center work free, and, of course, they are all women.

Organizations such as Feminists for Life are pro-woman and pro-life and work to make nurturance a social and political reality. Feminists for Life has publicized the fact that our nineteenth-century feminist foremothers were against abortion. In fact, they worked with physicians to restrict permissive abortion laws. Obviously, today, some extremists in the feminist movement have left behind their traditional roots and that complete commitment to nurturance for all.

Hazards of Reform Movements

In every reform movement, there are always those who fall into familiar traps. Some individuals struggling against oppression will identify with their oppressors: You have been thinking about and focusing on the enemy for so long, sometimes, you become the enemy. You begin to act in unjust ways, doing things that you once rebelled against. Others become separatists and give up the common tasks of bringing about unity and cooperation between opponents.

For some extremists in the feminist movement, the importance of female gender is overexaggerated. Feminine gender alone is thought to have effects on personal decision making. Others hold that women identifying with women can only flourish in women-to-women relationships. Unity of the sexes in love and work is rejected as undesirable and impossible. Such instances within the feminist movement betray the majority of women and deny our universal human nature. They also alienate younger generations of women.

A Look into the Twenty-First Century

The future of feminism and, in part, our culture will be decided by the importance placed upon gender by men and women in both thought and deed. My ideal future would include twin developments: (1) the positive strengths of the traditional feminine role must be recognized; and (2) development opportunities for women as unique individuals will be expanded.

Women who newly value and accept themselves as women can reach out and develop their talents, which go far beyond the undergirding feminine ideal. Women can take on more public leadership roles and learn to handle the conflicts and stress that go with their expanded roles as leaders, executives, and presiders. Women with new self-confidence can overcome the self-doubt and external limitations that have been imposed by the culture. I think most of the women I know have fought as many battles against their own self-doubt and belief in themselves as they have with external obstacles. I feel that a healthy, holistic emphasis upon individual personality and unique gifts develops once women are both secure and challenged to grow by new opportunities.

A utopian future would see the twenty-first century assimilate and incorporate the traditional feminine virtues of nurturing care while freeing individuals to grow in their own unique directions as persons. I have tried to capture this with an image: "At first, women were invisible, and now they are visible, so that is progress." However, there is something beyond being visible and that is being *transparent*. When one is transparent, gender does not define the whole self; rather, *who* one is as an individual person becomes the more important focus.

As part of this general assimilation, however, men must also be liberated to develop their nurturing qualities and family allegiances. The real test of my feminism was, I believe, how well I raised my five sons: What kind of a job did I do? What will they be like as adults? The ideal goal is to engender the development of fully mature persons, men and women of care and character who can love and work to sustain our civilization. As Christianity and feminism have always agreed, the whole person is far more than gender identity or gender role. Great and holy persons have always incorporated the virtues and strengths of both male and female.

Conclusion

In the future, women will contribute to culture in ways that are both traditional and new. We of this generation have begun a new adventure. We have been blessed; we have been living in the most interesting of times. We follow a Lord who makes all things new, and we can hope that men and women of the future will live in a culture transformed by feminine consciousness and nurturance. The coming of full equality of women can be a revolution that will increase joy, justice, and peace. Then, all manner of things will be well.

Model 3
One Tapestry: Many Voices, Many Colors
Diana Hayes

> And when we speak we are afraid
> our words will not be heard
> nor welcomed.
> But when we are silent
> we are still afraid.
>
> So it is better to speak
> remembering
> we were never meant to survive.
>
> (Audre Lorde, *Litany for Survival*)

The theme that runs throughout the readings for our Eucharist today is that of waiting: waiting in hope, often waiting in fear, too often waiting in silence. Waiting upon the One who has promised to come again, bringing a new reality, a new world—of peace, of love, of justice.

We are very good at waiting. As women, we have waited for centuries for our husbands, our fathers, our sons, our brothers—for all of the men in our lives—to listen to the message we bring, a message of love and peace, of justice and true equality, of the shared humanity of all God's creations, of hope in a truly shared life in Church and society. This is the message we, as women, have been the unheard and ignored bearers of from time immemorial. We have been waiting, with Mary Magdalene, since Christ's death and resurrection, for our words of wisdom to not only be heard but to be believed.

As the black feminist Audre Lorde points out [in the poem above], that waiting has been one fraught with tension, the tension of wondering whether and how our words will be received, of what the response will be: Will we be misunderstood? Will we be misrepresented? or Will we simply be ignored? Another part of that tension lies within ourselves. Do even we, ourselves, understand the message that we are attempting to proclaim? Part of me—as I look around at you this evening—says no, we do not. Because from where I stand, the wisdom of women that is being proclaimed is not very representative of my voice—the voice of a woman of color.

A Collective Wisdom

Too often, this wisdom of women, this precious gift and knowledge that we bear and seek to offer to the Church and to the world at large, reflects the perspective of only one group of women—white women. Yet, if we are to be heard, if we are to be recognized as truly prophetic voices, must we not ourselves recognize that women's wisdom is a collective wisdom, the collective wisdom of all women of the earth—be they black, brown, yellow, red, or white?

As the prophet Isaiah has stated: "Would that you might meet us doing right, that we were mindful of you in our ways!" That we would be cognizant of those missing voices, recognizing that without them, our message loses its harmony, is dimmed in its vibrant tapestry, and too quickly fades away into discord and disillusionment. The wisdom of women must be a multi-colored, multi-hued tapestry that startles those who behold it into a new consciousness, a new understanding of what it truly means to be one in Christ Jesus.

In the words of Audre Lorde once again:

> As women, we have been taught either to ignore our differences, or to view them as causes for separation and suspicion rather than as forces for change. Without community, there is no liberation, only the most vulnerable and temporary armistice between an individual and her oppression. But community must not mean a shedding of our difference, nor the pathetic pretense that these differences do not exist.
>
> Those of us who stand outside the circle of this society's definition of acceptable women; those of us who have been forged in the crucibles of difference—those of us who are poor... who are black, who are older—know that survival is not an academic skill. It is learning how to stand alone, unpopular and sometimes reviled, and how to make common cause with those others identified as outside the structure in order to define and seek a world in which we can all flourish ("The City of Freedom," *Sister Outsider: Essays and Speeches* [The Crossing Press, 1984], p. 112).

Our message loses its force if we cry out against inequity while perpetuating inequity within our midst. We must remember that our tapestry must be one of many voices, of many colors, of many perspectives. Only then will it truly be a tapestry—a weaving of the wisdom of all women. With that understanding amongst us, renewed and strengthened by each other, we will be able to speak out, despite our fears, despite the dangers, rejoicing in our differences and "remembering that we were never meant to survive." Each time I read or recite that phrase, it takes on new meaning for me. Tonight, I read its message as warning us of the dangers of silence.

Women and Their Witness

To remain silent in the face of injustice; to remain silent in the face of confusion and discord; to remain silent in the face of wars and rumors of wars; to remain silent when today's world appears hell-bent toward destruction; to remain silent when we have been commissioned, not simply by our baptism in Christ, but by Christ himself through Mary Magdalene at the tomb, is to condemn ourselves to lives of mere survival, of passive indifference, of sinful stoicism, of complicity in evil.

We are not meant simply to survive; we are meant to live, to live lives that witness, in their courageous stance against the evils in our midst, to the indwelling of the liberating spirit of the One who has come and will come again.

The coming of Christ was first revealed to a woman, Mary, the Mother of Jesus. The wondrous news of Jesus' victory over death was first revealed to women: Mary and her companions at the empty tomb. We do not know the appointed time or hour when Christ will come again. We must remain vigilant; we must be on guard for the signs of that coming.

Speaking in a Collective Voice

Yet, in our coming together, in our speaking out, in our coming to collective voice as women, can it be denied that we, once again, perhaps act as heralds of the good news of that coming—of the emergence of that new reality, that new dispensation in Christ Jesus?

If nothing else, with our voices raised in union calling for equitable justice in all walks of life, for men and women regardless of race or ethnicity, we will certainly keep the Church awake, vigilant, and alert!

Reflection Questions

1. Each of the three speakers addressed the theme of conversion from a personal perspective. How do their approaches to and experiences of conversion differ? Where are there common threads?

2. In what ways have you encountered the conversion experience in your life? How has this experience changed you?

3. What can you do in your local community to encourage conversion in the area of women and their concerns?

Model Panel Discussions

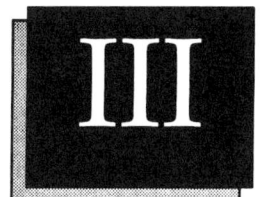

Panel discussions are a good way to cover several different points of view in a short time period. In addition, they offer a structured forum for exchanging information, ideas, and individual experiences. When developing a panel, be certain to choose your panel members with care; the mix should be eclectic, representing different experiences, backgrounds, and/or roles in the Church. This section offers two model panel discussions: (1) Forum on Women in the Diocesan Church and (2) Panel on Collaborative Ministry.

Panel 1: Forum on Women in the Diocesan Church

The first panel focuses on some areas of concern addressed by diocesan women's commissions. These concerns, for the most part, mirror those faced by women in society at large. The three panelists earned their badges in the forge of everyday experience, serving on women's commissions in their dioceses and archdioceses. The panelists include:

Joyce Cox, a Sister of Charity of the Blessed Virgin Mary, is vice chancellor and coordinator of religious in the Archdiocese of Seattle. She serves as liaison with the archdiocesan Commission on Women and also with the National Council of Catholic Women.

Judith O'Brien, a social worker, is co-chairperson of the Diocese of Rochester's Commission on Women.

Phyllis Willerscheidt is executive director of the Commission on Women in the Archdiocese of St. Paul and Minneapolis.

Panel 2: Collaborative Ministry

The second panel brings together three people who share ministry at St. Rose of Lima Parish in Gaithersburg, Maryland. Here, they present their views on collaborative church ministry: what it looks like; what makes it difficult to practice; and how their backgrounds contributed to their ability to work together. The panelists include:

Reverend Robert Duggan is pastor at St. Rose of Lima.

Maureen Kelly, now catechetical advisor to Silver Burdett & Ginn Publishers, is a former staff member at St. Rose of Lima.

Tara Seeley is a lawyer and director of outreach services at St. Rose of Lima.

Listening with Heart and Mind. Participant contemplates the many contributions of women to the Church.

Panel 1
Forum on Women in the Diocesan Church

What Our Commission on Women Does
Phyllis Willerscheidt

Our mission as a commission on women in St. Paul and Minneapolis is to serve as a prophetic voice for the future role of women in the Church. Let me quote from *Women: Pastoral Reflections,* written by the Minnesota bishops in March 1979:

> A woman who views herself as the image of God is conscious of her great dignity, a dignity that bestows self-acceptance and self-esteem. Holding this God-view toward herself and toward other women, she is called to extend this recognition outward to all people, enabling all to value and enhance each other's dignity as responsible and loving persons....
>
> Wherever, within the Church or society, a woman does not find liturgies, educational programs, social events or decision-making structures that meet her own and other's needs, she should work with persistence to establish them.

Our commission promotes justice, equality, love, healing, and empowerment of God's people, especially of archdiocesan women. My role is to serve as paid staff with the commission, joining in partnership with twenty-one volunteer commissioners, who meet to develop programs and plans and to look at future trends to further the role of women in the Church. We have committees that investigate various issues, and we serve as a research and study organization. Also, in my capacity as executive director, I get many calls from women who are upset with the Church for one reason or another and just need someone to listen to them.

Our commission is made up of lay men and women, priests, seminarians, and men and women religious; we are of diverse cultures and persuasions. The Commission on Women has seven committees: (1) spirituality; (2) diaconate; (3) inclusive language; (4) justice and equality; (5) planning and allocations; (6) communications; and (7) executive team.

Spirituality Committee. This committee works on the discovery of the spirituality of individual committee members and provides female models of worship for special events. Some events center on reconciliation. One, for example, dealt with physical violence done to women. At least one of our members is a survivor of incest, and she is sharing her experience to help the committee become more understanding and knowledgeable on this subject.

Diaconate Committee. This committee completed research on the issue of admitting women to the diaconate. We passed our findings on to the archbishop, who then sent them on to the Bishops' Committee on the Permanent Diaconate, National Conference of Catholic Bishops. We firmly believe that the diaconate offers an opportunity for women to contribute their gifts to the service of the Church.

Inclusive Language Committee. The use of inclusive language throughout the archdiocese is the work of this committee. It conducts language workshops and encourages writers of new songs to use appropriate language. We have adopted a model policy statement on inclusive language, which was adopted by the archdiocesan Pastoral Council in 1988 and by the Presbyteral Council in 1989, with some adaptations. The commission also produced a videotape called *Wholeness for the People of God,* which can be purchased or rented.

Justice and Equality Committee. This committee is responsive to women personnel in the Church. We have helped parish secretaries and office personnel to organize an association to further their spirituality and to network with one another. The committee is putting together a one-page brochure to assist parishes in helping women during crisis situations. We are listing emergency phone numbers to deal with problems related to physical abuse, chemical dependency, and family life situations. This is needed by pastors and parish secretaries because they often are the first ones contacted by women in trouble. Every five years, the committee distributes a survey that looks at leadership roles of women in the archdiocese. The results to date show that we are making strides at the archdiocesan level but are still dragging behind at the parish level. The committee also is putting together some guidelines to establish a scholarship fund for women who want to pursue some form of spiritual enrichment, whether it is a retreat or a formal classroom event. We have found that there are many funds for men but not many for women. We now have a $1500 grant from a parish to help women.

Planning and Allocations Committee. This committee provides planning for the commission and helps with the commission's budget requests for various programs.

Communications Committee. Part of the committee's responsibility is to publish a quarterly newsletter that promotes love, healing, and empowerment of women. Our upcoming issue will be on the subject of healing.

Executive Team Committee. This committee functions as a participatory body to make decisions for the commission between meetings. We are trying to model for the archdiocese an alternative management design, based on the female-style of management.

Let me conclude by noting that archdiocesan women believe in working tirelessly—until women within the Church are treated with love and equality for the gifts they have to share with all the people of God.

Rochester's Commission on Women
Judith O'Brien

The Rochester Commission on Women comes out of a truly unique history. Recall that Rochester, New York, was the home of Susan B. Anthony and Frederick Douglass, while Elizabeth Cady Stanton was from nearby Geneva. Given the history of women in our diocese, it is no surprise that a pastoral on women was written for the Rochester church in 1982.

Ours is one of the oldest diocesan women's commissions, and its birth is a direct result of women praying, studying, and planning together. The commission was established in response to two seminal events: locally, in 1982, the publication of *The Fire in the Thornbush*; and nationally, in 1983, the U.S. Catholic bishops' decision to write a pastoral on women. Since its founding in 1985, our commission has formed its mission, objectives, and activities in light of these two significant events.

How Our Commission Works

In 1987, commission members wrote a charter and a mission statement. As I recall, they drove to Seneca Falls to use the library of the National Women's Hall of Fame to discuss and write the document. Our mission says that the commission on women was formed "to help create and sustain a climate of openness to the gifts and potential of all women as well as to the needs and hurts of those women who today are working for equal discipleship in the Church." Mission statements force us to try our best to state the reasons for our existence; to identify those with whom we have chosen to work and to serve; and to provide the framework for goals, planning, and priorities.

Commission Membership

Twenty members make up our commission. Each person serves no more than six years. As vacancies occur, members are asked to submit names to the bishop, who makes the final selection. Since we are a diocesan body, our membership attempts to be representative of the diocese's various regions and groups. We find this requirement challenging and frustrating because when we try to have a good mix of people, it is difficult to find common meeting times, reasonable travel distances, and so forth. Even so, in recent years, we have had fairly good ethnic and minority representation.

Leadership

Two years ago the commission changed its executive leadership structure from a hierarchic model of chairperson, vice chairperson, and secretary to a collaborative team model. The result is that each year we elect six members as the leadership team: two conveners, who also are spokespersons for the commission, and four persons to monitor the work of our four standing committees: (1) ministry and spirituality; (2) social justice and advocacy; (3) education; and (4) communications and public relations.

As a small budgeted program with a support staff shared by six other special diocesan pastoral ministries, our commission exercises a broad range of responsibility as the major advisor to our bishop on diocesan women and their concerns. We are a deliberative body, which means that there is always discussion, planning for follow-through, and decision making during monthly committee and team leadership meetings. Our decision-making process is based on a consensus model.

Activities

We assist our bishop as needed in his work with the NCCB Committee on Women in Society and in the Church. On a regular basis, we meet with the bishop to go over the work of the commission and to be updated by him. Our current areas of concern include the following:

- women's ministry preparation needs, including financial and vocational; and
- the rising expectations that result from the increasing awareness of sexism in the Church and in society.

Our accomplishments include the following:

- establishing an endowed scholarship fund for women studying theology and ministry at St. Bernard's Institute;
- organizing listening sessions between women who are preparing for ministry and women in ministry;
- continuing dialogue with the Priests' Council, suggesting common areas of support and collaboration such as input to the upcoming diocesan synod;
- cosponsoring a fund-raising/educational benefit for Mary's Pence, which will include participation by women from innercity parishes; and
- holding regular meetings with the diocesan director of the Office of the Diaconate, offering suggestions for improved relationships between deacons and women in ministry.

In conclusion, let me note that commissions by definition are created to fulfill a need for consultation in a particular area of interest. Consultation and advice are arrived at after deliberation. Diocesan commissions on women, consequently, must meet often and know how to move from talk to written recommendations. Members need to be skilled in communication and consensus building. Finally, when they deliberate and advise, commissions must be taken seriously by those whom they advise.

Seattle's Commission on Women
Sister Joyce Cox

The roots of the Commission on Women in the Archdiocese of Seattle go back to 1980 and the 600th anniversary of the death of St. Catherine of Siena. This event prompted Archbishop Raymond Hunthausen to write a pastoral statement on women. In it he said:

> I chose this anniversary year as the pastoral head of the church of western Washington to address the issue of women in the Church. While I am acutely aware that the degree of conflict and dissatisfaction is not the same for all women, I do wish to understand and be sensitive to all and to educate all in the basic Christian truths as they relate to the situation on women. In this spirit, I address this letter to all women and men of the Church of western Washington.

Archbishop Hunthausen's goal was to have a women's commission that could be advisory but also could help monitor the goals that the archdiocese and the pastoral council were putting into action. In reflection, I would like to enumerate some of those goals that the archbishop hoped would bring equality for women into decision-making processes and into the archdiocesan church.

Archdiocesan Goals for Equality

1. An affirmative action plan for leadership and consultation in all parish and diocesan departments and agencies.
2. Equal access for women and men to theological and pastoral education consistent with their capabilities.
3. Giving full cooperation and support to the National Conference of Catholic Bishops' Committee on Worship to eliminate sexist language and imagery from all official church documents, catechisms, liturgical books, hymns, and rituals.
4. Elimination of sexist language and imagery from all parish and diocesan and department communications.
5. Equal employment opportunities and equal compensation for qualified women and men in church positions.

6. Active recruitment of women as lectors and ministers of the eucharist with provision of training programs where such programs do not exist presently.
7. Active recruitment of qualified women to serve on archdiocesan and pastoral councils, boards, and committees.
8. Active recruitment of qualified women to serve in full professional capacities on archdiocesan and parish teams in ministries of family counseling, liturgy development, and social justice.

Initially, eight women from western Washington were asked to work on the newly formed women's commission, along with the pastoral council and the archbishop, to implement those goals.

Mission Statement

The women's first mission statement stated that all archdiocesan women and men were co-creators in building God's community in our Church and in our world. "We are a group of persons dedicated to the task of empowering women for full integration in all areas of church life," the statement continued. "As the archdiocese's Women's Commission, we are committed to actions that will support, educate, and call forth the gifts of both women and men in the church of western Washington, thus challenging the faith community to a new vision of Church and person."

It soon became evident that the women's commission needed a broader representation, people not only from the Seattle area, but also from the entire archdiocese. The commission used advertising to recruit more people to its ranks, in the diocesan paper, in archdiocesan weekly mailings to all the parishes, and in church bulletins. Fourteen women and men, representing the diocese, were chosen to be on the commission.

Composition of the Commission on Women

There were one or two men on the commission; the rest were married, single, and religious women. They saw themselves as advocates for women and the roles of women. And, they saw themselves empowered to do more than be advisory. To be more than advisory, there had to be a means of eliciting the understanding, the storytelling, from women and men in the various areas of church life, as well from as those who felt disenfranchised.

Gaining Visibility

It was 1984 before the women's commission came to have real visibility. This was done through sponsoring listening sessions throughout the archdiocese. The regional listening sessions were an educational opportunity for men and women to gather and have their consciousness raised about women's issues and contributions.

Then, when the request came for help with the first draft of the U.S. bishops' pastoral on women, it was the archdiocesan women's commission that was asked to coordinate the process. All the information that came in from the last six listening sessions in the archdiocese went into the *Partners in the Mystery of Redemption,* the first draft of the pastoral. We had a lot of responses and collated all the material and sent it to Bishop Imesch and his committee.

The women's commission also put the names of all those who had attended the listening sessions into a computer so we had a networking data bank of about 700 men and women. The idea was to facilitate communication easily, whenever needed.

Reflection Questions

1. Reflect carefully on the areas of concern addressed by the model panel. Now, think of your local situation. In which areas do you think a commission on women would be most useful for your diocese? Why?

2. What groups and organizations are there in your parish and in your diocese that address women's concerns? Are they accomplishing their goals and objectives? How?

3. What can you do personally to be supportive of women and their concerns?

Panel 2
Collaborative Ministry

Who Does Team Ministry?

The panelists opened the discussion by describing their backgrounds and relating what they consider to be the major influences on their religious development, both while growing up and in their first years in ministry.

MAUREEN KELLY: I am a great believer that our family of origin has a lot to do with the kind of persons we become as ministers. I also feel that we need to consider that aspect more seriously in our reflection, as well as in some of the things that are occurring for us in pain and in hope in Church today.

My family was not stereotypical of Irish-Catholic families in the 1940s and 1950s. My grandmother, who lived with us and was an Irish immigrant, worked. My mother worked, and my father worked. My father was able to deal with flexible roles. I watched my dad cook, go to the grocery store, take us to the doctor; and I watched my mother and my grandmother do the same things.

I grew up in Buffalo, New York, in a white, Irish-Catholic "ghetto." I thought that God was white, Irish, and Catholic until, at age twenty-eight, I went to Louvain University in Belgium and studied theology. I was the oldest of five children and, until I was sixteen, the only girl in the family. My father was the nurturer of faith, the one who was more involved in the Church. My father got my mother into Christian Family Movement and took us to Notre Dame to the CFM convention every summer.

My mother, though, gave us much more of a sense of mission. My mother was the family politician. She was the first woman in New York State to receive the "Man of the Year" award for a political party, which will go unnamed. From my late teens until twenty-seven, I was a member of a religious community, and that has certainly been a constituent part of my development, my spirituality, and my experience of living day to day with women.

After that, I worked in the public school system in Buffalo with emotionally disturbed minority children. It was also at that time that I came to be a volunteer in parish ministry because priests I had gone to grade school and high school with asked me if I would please come and train their CCD teachers.

ROBERT DUGGAN: I will tell you a bit about me, about who I am. I am from an Irish-Catholic family, with five brothers and sisters. My father was a convert, but not particularly pious. My mother was the one with lots of religion in the family; on her side, I have all sorts of cousins in the Church, ranging from a bishop and a monsignor to religious women in vows.

For the most part, we were brought up in a very traditional Catholic family. We travelled a lot and lived in various parts of the country, even overseas. We were the type of family that would search for a parochial school first and then shop for a house in the parish; priests came to dinner at our house.

When I graduated from Catholic high school, I entered the seminary, attending one of the grand old seminaries in this country, St. Charles in Catonsville, Maryland, and then St. Mary's in Baltimore. After that, I went to the North American College in Rome for four years of theology and was ordained in 1970. I came home to the Archdiocese of Washington, where I have been a priest for twenty years.

Most of my priestly ministry has been in parish settings, primarily in affluent, suburban parishes. I have had relatively little exposure to working with other ethnic groups or cultures. I think I am a fairly typical mainstream cleric in the American Church today. However, I have probably had the opportunity to do some specialized things that many parish priests have not had, including some writing and speaking around the country on the topic of the RCIA, which was my area of specialization during graduate studies. But most of my time and energy over the last twenty years have been spent trying to figure out what makes parishes work and how to work in parishes.

TARA SEELEY: Who I am in ministry is very much shaped by the era in which I was born. I was born in 1956, so only my early sacramental preparation was prior to the Second Vatican Council. Listening to Bob's story, I realize that we are actually in a multicultural ministry, because I do not know the culture in which he was raised; it has not been part of my own experience.

As a family, we regularly went to Catholic parishes, and we also moved around a lot. My father was Protestant, and my mother was Catholic and committed to raising us as Catholics. She was also committed to keeping us in the public schools. So, my formation has been through CCD and religious education programs, as they were trying to shape themselves in response to church renewal.

A large part of my formation for ministry has been in ecumenical studies and settings; their vision of small-group prayer and study and their call to leadership in the community are very dear to me. St. Rose's is the first parish in which I have ministered. But if you accept the theory that a group changes each time someone leaves or comes in, I have worked on thirteen parish staffs because of the turnover we have had.

Wisdom Figures and Partnership

MAUREEN KELLY: As I look back on my own experience of partnership with men in ministry and also in business, there were several constitutive experiences that shaped me. One was watching how my mother and father related and communicated and struggled and articulated and were intimate and how they involved us in the decision-making process of what it meant to be a family. From watching how my father related to my grandmother and to my mother, I began to have a sense of self, a sense of what it meant to be a woman and also of what it meant to be a woman in a mostly male world. My father taught us to believe that we could do anything we wanted to do. There was never a word like he "let" us do things. My father taught me very early that I had to stand my ground with the boys.

The second constitutive experience for me was going to the seminary in Belgium in 1972. I was the only woman in my class. That experience was a liminal experience, I think, for all of us. You are vulnerable together. You also learn together a sense of equality. There was a lot of pain there, but there also was a real experience of the beginning of partnership and of knowing that one has to commit oneself to vulnerability and risk and openness. If those elements are not there on either side, partnership will not occur.

I want to mention two clerics who stand out most in shaping my idea of ministry. The first one is Bishop John Sullivan, now the bishop of the Diocese of Kansas City—St. Joseph. The other is Father Bob Duggan. What I sensed both men had in common was a vision of Church and mission that was important to me. The other thing that they had in common was a way of involving women in decision making. I worked with Bishop Sullivan in Grand Island, Nebraska, on the diocesan level, and then I worked with him again in Kansas

City, Missouri. When my office proposed something, I was supported; I was listened to. I have experienced the same thing with Bob on a parish level. His approach was: This is your job description; this is what you are in charge of. We will talk about it, and we will make a decision that both of us together can support.

TARA SEELEY: One piece of wisdom that I bring to partnership in ministry is the wisdom of a woman who was a law student with me. We endured a very hostile environment that was not open to women. At a particularly painful time, she looked at me and said, "Just remember, your reality is not their reality," meaning that women's experience and women's reality, which have been denied in the wider culture where men are dominant, are something to be treasured, something to be held forth, something to be shared wisely. A positive way to say this is remember your own story and trust your own experience as a woman.

Another piece of wisdom that I bring to partnership is the wisdom of Sister Thea Bowman—what I call the wisdom of the earth and sea. In a *60 Minutes* piece done several years ago, the interviewer pressed her on her exclusion from preaching and the ordained ministry. She just laughed and said, "Why do I need permission to preach? I can preach on the bus; I can preach in the schoolyard; I will preach in the neighborhood; I will preach in the grocery store." I took from that the wisdom of the urgency of the mission.

There are two important moments that catalyzed, for me, my Roman Catholic identity. I was in college, at a small Episcopal school that was experiencing poor campus ministry by the local priest. Two adults in the community took the responsibility to call us Catholics together and, through their lives and witness, they showed us that the life of the community was the responsibility of all of us, that the pastoral care of the community belongs to us.

The other catalyst was a short and simple thing. Listening to public radio, I heard an ad promoting the U.S. bishops' Campaign for Human Development. It was the first time that I had ever heard about the campaign. That brief message about human dignity resonated so deeply with the values I had been raised with that it sparked, I think, a deeper love and loyalty for my own faith tradition.

ROBERT DUGGAN: My personal experience of partnership has been an experience of discovery in the giftedness and, in particular, the wisdom of women in mission. One of the exciting things about my time at St. Rose has been discovering the potential of collaborative ministry and true partnership. We have both men and women—lay, professed religious, and ordained—on our team at St. Rose, and it has been a spectacularly invigorating experience for me personally to share in a vision of Church with my co-workers. As I look back over my ministry, I see there were many experiences of partnership. Let me mention several.

At my second parish, there was a married woman, Linda Carr, who was the director of religious education. She and I were soulmates in developing a vision of renewal for a parish that was under the leadership of a strong and good pastor. She taught me a lot of

Women's Commissions at Work.
During the Forum on Women in the Diocesan Church, panelists address the issues, concerns, and activities of local women's commissions.

fundamental things about the complexities of trying to collaborate with someone who has a home, a family, a spouse, and so forth, and about the need to shift expectations regarding the nature of collaboration in ministry when someone is not—as I am—involved night and day in that ministry.

I think also of my early experience in an ecumenical context with Shalem, which is an ecumenically based group in Washington, D.C., devoted to spiritual development and formation experiences. Working very intensely in spiritual formation experiences in that context opened for me a whole world of insight.

As I reflect on partnership, I have to mention the enormous generosity of the volunteers that I have met. The countless men and mostly women who make the Church in the United States run, who give billions of volunteer hours annually to make our Church what I think it is: one of the most vital churches in our tradition in the world. I am in awe and constantly humbled at the selflessness of people who juggle job, family, and civic involvements and still manage to be there when needed, and who keep challenging pastor and staff. It is a sacred chapter of our Church's history, and that sense of partnership with those people whose names I could list by the hundreds has left an indelible impression on me. That is the true meaning of partnership.

From those experiences and people, I discovered that I, the professional minister, had to become the learner. That has taught me a lifelong lesson: my most invigorating times in ministry are the times when I am working with people better than me, who challenge me and who teach me.

Stumbling Blocks on the Way to Partnership

MAUREEN KELLY: A lot of my pain has come from other women and other lay people with whom I have worked both, at a diocesan level and at a parish level. One of the most painful moments of my life was when I was leaving a parish and I received a letter from another woman with whom I was working. The letter said, "I am sorry that while you were here I sabotaged your ministry. I just did not like you." I would have liked to have heard that early on because I think that partnership in ministry means we could have dealt with it.

ROBERT DUGGAN: The most painful thing on my list, is my own awareness of my position of privilege because I am male, a cleric, well educated, and, though not personally affluent, I certainly have affluence at my disposal. I am constantly reminded of that. My business manager in the parish is a woman. I cannot tell you how many times she has called the archdiocesan offices and run into a brick wall because the person that she is dealing with says, "Well, I would like to speak to your pastor about that"; or she has been turned down cold, and I have to rescue the situation by using my power, my privilege, my status.

TARA SEELEY: One thing that is painful to me is that, while I am enjoying collaboration in a situation where I have pastoral responsibility and am able to use my gifts fully and freely, there is no systemic change in the church structure. I know countless women who cannot get hired in their diocese, who will not be asked to serve on diocesan commissions, who are shut out of participation in the Church. Another painful part, and this is more a challenge, has been claiming and/or celebrating my own charisms for ministry. St. Rose's is my first parish ministry. The model of parish ministry that I have in the Roman Catholic Church is the celibate male. I am a married woman, and in the last year, I have become a new mother. At first, it was very hard for me to have another model of ministry. I have had to carve out and claim, as gifts and strengths, the demands and realities of my life as a wife and a mother and that is an area in which I am still growing. The challenge for me in partnership has been to bring those aspects of my life to parish ministry as assets, not as liabilities.

Reflection Questions

1. You have listened to the panelists as they described their experiences with partnership ministry. Reflecting on what they have said, what would you identify as the three primary ingredients of successful team ministry? Why?

2. What has been your most successful experience of partnership? What was your least successful partnership experience? What do think made the difference between the two?

3. In your parish or diocese, where would you like to see more partnership in ministry? What can you do to help bring this to fruition?

Open Forum

This section features a selection of comments and questions that were raised in the symposium workshops. The questions illustrate some of the practical problems and concerns being dealt with by women and men in society and in the Church. The first set was presented to the Forum on Women in the Diocesan Church. The second set was presented to the Panel on Collaborative Ministry. Some of the questions from workshops are followed by answers from the panels. These are intended to give you an idea of how women's commissions and church leaders are responding creatively in the face of some vital issues affecting women today. You are invited to use these questions and to add to them in planning your own discussions and workshops.

Women Speak of Their Concerns
Questions Presented to
the Forum on Women in the Diocesan Church

Workshop 1:   Reaching Out to Immigrants

Q. Are we, as a Church, truly accepting of the cultural pluralism that is the fact of our Church today? What is our attitude as a people of God? as ministers? Are we accepting the gospel mandate to welcome the stranger so that there are no alienated strangers? We see that other Churches are effectively reaching out to, taking care of, listening to, and administrating to people who come to this country. Are we, as a Catholic Church, doing that sufficiently? Are we responding to pastoral needs? Also, we are concerned about the problem of implementation. We have marvelous structures in our Church to respond to the needs of newcomers, but, are we really reaching the grass-roots level? In all practicality, are the people actually able to welcome the stranger in our Church today?

A. Two weeks ago, the director of our Multicultural Ministries Office came to the women's commission and talked about many of the very same issues that you just outlined. It became obvious that if the women's commission does not model membership from all of the representative cultures, how can it really be in touch with the issues? We have to model that multicultural diversity in our agencies and our commissions and on all levels of the Church itself.

Workshop 2: Single-Parent Families

Q. How can the Church, especially through women's commissions, begin to identify and meet the needs of women in single-parent families?

A. These difficult issues surface a lot through diocesan-sponsored programs that deal with marriage preparation, the separated or divorced, and families coping with various problems. However, there is this concern that we never do enough. I think that the issues we are talking about here today seem to reflect the almost "crisis" situations we are experiencing in many communities today. Perhaps, commissions need to decide whether the single-parent family issue should be a priority for them, and whether or not they have the time and resources to address it adequately.

Workshop 3: Racism and Sexism— Factors in the Feminization of Poverty

Q. What can women's commissions do to make certain that all offices and dioceses are working on the problems of racism and sexism? It should not be the responsibility of just the Office of Black Catholics, or just the Women's Commission. However, the Women's Commission can hold the other offices accountable. We also talked about the need to work actively on public policies that protect women and that help women to achieve higher salaries, whether it be by changing jobs or career fields in which they have experienced discrimination, or through pay equity.

A. One way our diocese is handling this is to put sexism and racism on the agenda of the archbishop's all-staff meetings. We are going to take the issue to the full staff, offering in-service training sessions on sexism and racism, which we hope will heighten everyone's awareness of the need to address this issue.

Workshop 4: Single Women in Church and Society

Q. We would like to see dioceses establish a funded commission for women that would represent single women at all levels. However, if a commission is not feasible, why couldn't dioceses utilize already existing offices and organizations to address such issues as the feminization of poverty; the need to empower single women so that they can voice their own needs; the dilemma of gifted women who recognize the need to bear fruit, and yet whose gifts are not recognized?

Workshop 5: Women as Caretakers

Q. One concern we have is that the institutional Church can drain the energy of women by asking them to meet crisis needs as volunteers—both as care-givers in parishes and as family care-givers. Our feeling is that care-giving is not a feminine role but, rather, a human role that can be discerned just like any job. How can women's commissions support, encourage, and provide opportunities for such discernment? What other creative ways might your commissions be considering to provide support systems for those care-givers?

Women Speak of Their Concerns
Questions Presented to
the Panel on Collaborative Ministry

Workshop 1: Women in Canon Law

Q. We would encourage diocesan women's commissions to provide either an educational experience or workshop opportunities for women on the 1983 *Code of Canon Law* and its implications for women in the mission and ministry of the Church. The Code presents an enhanced role for the laity and that provides a framework for looking at the participation of women and the teaching, sanctifying, and governing functions of the Church. What might women's commissions do to recognize the rights of the Christian faithful as they are defined in the Code, and as they might apply to the role of women in the Church?

A. Wherever the Code includes or allows women, women's commissions should, with their bishops, put women in those places. This includes decision-making roles and consultative roles, so that women are participating fully throughout all levels of our diocesan structures.

Workshop 2: A Call to Ministry—
Women Administrators of Priestless Parishes

Q. What can diocesan women's commissions do to support and encourage women administrators of priestless parishes?

A. One of the things that we do not talk about enough is the importance of networking and support groups for women, by women, and with women. A chief source of nurturing and support for women in difficult situations comes from other women.

Workshop 3: Inclusive Family Ministry

COMMENT. We talked about the need to be aware of the changing face of the Church. In the year 2000, the Church in the United States will be 50 percent Hispanic. We need to find ways to move out of our more traditional middle-class view of things to be more welcoming to other people. Also, we recognize that there is a tremendous load on single parents and families that are in crisis. The economic situation is really strapping many families. We need things like daycare to bolster parents' efforts to give their values to their children. We need support groups for these people, probably peer groups, because it is those who are hurting who seem to be the most active in helping each other.

Workshop 4: Mary, a Woman for All Seasons

Q. What is being done at parish and diocesan levels to develop and foster a healthy, viable, devotion to Mary for women today?

A. A contemporary prayer resource that introduces people to the best of the Marian tradition, which can be used at all levels of parish life, is from *Pax Christi*. It is a very simple reflection on the role of

Mary as the mother of Jesus and on his role as Prince of Peace. It is the Mary of the *Magnificat* who announces the justice of God and the end of oppression, and it puts us in touch with her realization of the great things that God has done.

Reflection Questions

1. What issues or questions would you like to see discussed by local women's commissions, either on the parish or the diocesan level?

2. When you look at the range of issues addressed by women's commissions, what do you consider to be the most pressing need in your local community?

3. What would you consider to be the three most important concerns to your parish or diocese? Why?

4. Of those three concerns, which are you presently working on in your local area? How?

Workshops in Action

Workshops can take a variety of different shapes and forms. No one pattern is the "right" or the "best" one for a particular group's needs. In this section, we offer several workshop models, all based on those held during The Wisdom of Women Symposium.

The first three workshops—women in canon law; pro-life and feminism; and women's spirituality—use the pattern of presentation, followed by discussion. The workshop on women and aging uses an outline form—a form that might be adapted to fit your local needs and setting. The models presented here are meant to assist you in developing similar workshops in your diocese or local community. In addition, we have included a list of workshop topics that proved of interest to symposium participants. It is hoped that they might spark your creativity when planning your own workshop or seminar on women in society and in the Church.

The Presenters

Helen Alvaré is an attorney and a theologian, currently serving as the director of planning and information with the NCCB Secretariat for Pro-Life Activities. Her presentation is based on remarks she made at the workshop in which she participated. She focuses on whether the pro-life movement embodies feminist principles and on how true feminism supports life at all stages, especially in its very earliest stage within the woman's womb.

55

Sister Sharon Euart, RSM, is a canon lawyer and associate general secretary at the National Conference of Catholic Bishops/United States Catholic Conference. Her canon law text compares the 1917 *Code of Canon Law* with the revised Code of 1983. Sr. Euart's emphasis is on showing how much latitude the new Code gives to women within the Church. She says the Code's bill of rights for laity should be used to the fullest to involve women in the life and mission of the Church. Her text is based closely on her presentation at the symposium.

Dana Greene is a professor of history at St. Mary's College in Maryland and a graduate of the Shalem Institute for Spiritual Formation. She is the author of a biography of Evelyn Underhill, the English lay woman who pioneered the spirituality of ordinary life. Dr. Greene treats the topic of spirituality and women. Drawing on her experiences with spiritual formation, she suggests that women's spirituality may take a unique path, based on women's unique experiences. Rather than a fully developed text, she offers stimulus for discussion.

Workshop Model 1
Women in Canon Law
Sister Sharon Euart, RSM

The awareness on the part of the fathers of the Second Vatican Council of the role of women in society and in the Church has expanded and intensified over the last twenty-five years. Reflecting this experience, Pope John Paul II's *Christifideles Laici* states that "it is necessary that the Church recognize all the gifts of men and women for her life and mission and put them into practice." Taking the teaching of the Council further, Pope John Paul II goes on to say that "the acknowledgment in theory of the active and responsible presence of women in the Church must be realized in practice." Such realization, suggests the papal exhortation, finds expression in the revised *Code of Canon Law* and its provisions on the participation of women in the life and mission of the Church. Among those provisions mentioned in *Christifideles Laici* are participation on parish and diocesan pastoral councils, diocesan synods, catechesis, and transmission of the Word of God through study, research, and theological teaching.

In citing the *Code of Canon Law* as a source for "putting into practice" what is theoretically permissible for the active and responsible participation of women in the life and mission of the Church, Pope John Paul II urges a closer, more careful reading of the revised law. It is to this review that I would like to direct my remarks today.

1917 *Code of Canon Law*

The 1983 *Code of Canon Law* represents a shift in the Church's perspective on the role of women in the Church and has altered significantly the juridic or legal condition of women. Under the former Code (1917), although no canon explicitly defined the inferior legal status of women, numerous norms limited the participation of women in the teaching, sanctifying, and governing mission of the Church.

The Church's negative view of women characterized her as (1) subordinate to a man; (2) an occasion of sin to man and seductive; (3) intellectually inferior and lacking sound judgment; and (4) timid, scrupulous, and in need of protection. Based on the principle that law is generally understood to follow life rather than to create it, such a treatment of women was influenced by perspectives on women derived from philosophical and theological thought that prevailed in particular historical periods.

Several canons in the 1917 Code presented a passive and inferior role for women in liturgical functions (cc. 314.2, 813, 910.2, 1262); others reflected an understanding of woman as subordinate to her husband in marriage (cc. 1112, 1223.2). Some canons implied that women were sinful or dangerous by prohibiting their physical proximity to men, particularly to the celibate clergy (c. 133); others excluded women from administrative and judicial roles in the Church (cc. 1520, 1521).

Second Vatican Council

With the Second Vatican Council, a notable shift has taken place. Conciliar documents, papal statements, statements of individual bishops, synodal statements, and other ecclesial documents manifest a different understanding of women and provide a perspective that differs from the one found in the 1917 Code. They all speak persuasively to the principle of equality. This newer understanding is based on the conciliar teaching that the Church is the people of God (see *Lumen Gentium*, 11, 14), a holy people incorporated into the Body of Christ by baptism (Ibid., 11), with a share in the threefold mission of Christ to teach, to sanctify, and to govern (Ibid., 31).

All members of the Church share a common dignity, the same vocation to holiness. They enjoy a fundamental equality that arises from baptism in Christ (Ibid., 32) that precedes any differentiation on the basis of diversity of functions. Thus, the Council emphasized that there is one people of God, but many forms of service.

The teaching of the Second Vatican Council did not take place within a vacuum. The Council fathers were also influenced by the "signs of the times" and by the changing role of women in society that was taking place throughout the world. Shifts in patterns of relationship between men and women in marriage and in family life, legal protections in the workplace and in education, and a new awareness of sexism in virtually every social structure—including the Church—are examples of changes of the past twenty-five years that have affected women's roles in society and influenced, to a certain extent, the changing role of women in the Church.

In the context of the conciliar teaching, women are acknowledged as equal in dignity to men, inherently good, and endowed with intellect, judgment, and initiative. It is within this framework that the role of women in the Church has undergone change. And, generally speaking, it is this understanding of women and women's role in the Church that is reflected in the revised law of the Church.

1983 *Code of Canon Law*

The positive representation of women in the 1983 Code is due primarily to the enhanced position of the laity in the revised law. The revised Code's acknowledgment of a proper role for the laity in the mission and ministry of the Church has helped, if only minimally, to advance the role of women in the Church.

To direct the process for revising the universal law of the Church, Pope Paul VI proposed ten principles for revision that were approved by the Synod of Bishops in 1967. These principles were to serve as guidelines for the process of revising the entire Code of Canon Law. Principle No. 6 identified the "fundamental equality of all members of the Christian faithful" as a common juridic status and urged that "the rights of persons be appropriately defined and safeguarded." As a result, when the canons [of the 1983 Code] refer to "laity" and "Christian faithful," women are included in that designation.

Let us take a look at some of the specific changes in the revised law that provide for increased participation of women in the mission and ministry of the Church. It is in the context of Church ministry that I would like to review such changes. Without getting into the ongoing debate over the definition of ministry in the Church, I would suggest for our purposes today a broad usage of the notion of ministry and an organization of three categories: (1) common, (2) public, and (3) jurisdictional.

Common Ministry

Common ministry, that which is proper to all the Christian faithful, includes such activities as love of neighbor, evangelization in one's own way, and building up the Church according to one's gifts. Examples of common ministry that are proper to lay men and women and that are recognized by the Code include proclaiming the Gospel, especially in circumstances where only the lay person can effectively do so (c. 225.1); transforming the temporal order with the spirit of the Gospel (c. 225.2); and promoting the upbuilding of the Church through marriage and family life (c. 226).

Public Ministry

In addition to such instances of common ministry proper to the laity in the world, the Code also recognizes that lay men and women can be called by ecclesiastical authorities to offices and works within the Church and hence to what is called *public ministry*, a form of ministry within the Church that requires some type of designation from ecclesiastical authority. Examples include religion teacher, director of religious education, eucharistic minister, parish council president, and parish visitor of the sick.

The 1983 Code, in addressing functions and works within the Church, adopts the Council's broad sense of ecclesiastical office and defines it as "any function constituted in a stable manner by divine or ecclesiastical law to be exercised for a spiritual purpose" (c. 145.1). The Code's definition of ecclesiastical office reflects the notions that lay men and women might be deputed by the hierarchy for certain roles to be carried out for a spiritual purpose and that bishops might commit offices to lay men and women for the service of the Church.

Under the 1917 Code, ecclesiastical office was reserved to the ordained, but since Vatican II, it has become clear that lay men and women may hold office in the Church. This redefinition and expansion of the notion of ecclesiastical office represents one of the most substantive and significant changes in the 1983 Code, for it provides a framework for increased participation of lay men and women in the teaching, sanctifying, and governing mission of the Church.

While all ministry that requires some type of recognition by ecclesiastical authority might be called public ministry, the term *official ministry* might be used to designate only those ministries that pertain to an ecclesiastical office, recognizing, of course, that this does not reflect the full range of ecclesial ministries in which lay men and women are serving. In other words, all ministries in which lay men and women are serving in the Church are not necessarily roles that have been designated as ecclesiastical offices.

The Code clearly recognizes some "official" ministries that, with ecclesiastical authorization, may be assumed by lay men and women:

> ***Teaching Office.*** A lay person, hence a woman, may assist the pastor in the parish catechetical ministry (c. 776), serve as catechist in missionary lands to teach on behalf of the Church (c. 785), and teach the sacred sciences in institutions of higher learning (c. 229.3).

Sanctifying Office. A lay man or woman may serve as liturgical minister in performing the functions of lector, commentator, and cantor (c. 230.2), special minister of the eucharist (cc. 230.3, 910.2), and minister of sacramentals (c. 1168). Only a lay man, however, may be installed (that is, by means of a liturgical service) as lector or acolyte (c. 230.1). It is interesting to note that many of the liturgical functions that lay men and women may perform are permitted only when there is a priest or deacon lacking. It would seem that roles associated with the sanctifying function of the Church are still primarily thought of in terms of clergy.

Governing Office. A lay person, man or woman, may serve in the tribunal ministries of auditor (c. 1428), assessor (c. 1424), promoter of justice and defender of the bond (c. 1435). Administratively, a lay person may be chancellor and notary for cases not involving clerics (c. 483.2). A lay person may also serve as diocesan financial officer (c. 494.1), member of a parish pastoral team (c. 517.2), and secretary general of the episcopal conference (c. 451). Within lay religious institutes, superiors (cc. 617, 620, 621), councilors (c. 627), financial officers (c. 636), and novice directors (c. 651) also exercise official ministries.

Also in the area of governance, there are consultative functions open to the lay men and women: membership on plenary and provincial councils (c. 443.3,.5); diocesan synods (c. 463); diocesan pastoral (c. 512) and finance (c. 492) councils; and parish pastoral (c. 536) and finance (c. 537) councils. In addition, the pope can call to an ecumenical council those whom he wishes and determine the degree of participation (c. 339.2). All of these functions are established by universal ecclesiastical law, possess objective stability and a spiritual purpose, and can thus be considered official ministries.

Additional offices, and consequently official ministries, constituted by particular ecclesiastical law, that is, the law of a local Church, may vary from diocese to diocese. Functions such as diocesan director of liturgy, parish directors of religious education, and principals of Catholic schools, as well as members of parish pre-Cana teams that are stably established according to diocesan guidelines (cc. 1063, 1064) could be included in particular ecclesiastical law as official ministry.

Although the ministries I have just mentioned require some type of recognition by ecclesiastical authority for their public exercise, it need not be by means of a conferral of office. Very often, and perhaps in most dioceses, the diocesan bishop chooses not to establish offices formally, but prefers to direct and coordinate ecclesial ministries in less formal ways such as through the use of guidelines, policies, or specific directives.

Thus, it is clear that the 1983 Code provides opportunities for the participation of women in a number of functions that are public and require some type of recognition from ecclesiastical authority, which could be, but need not be, established as ecclesiastical offices.

Jurisdictional Ministry

Although public ministry, both official and unofficial (not attached to an ecclesiastical office), is available to the laity, there is difficulty in determining which functions can be entrusted to lay men and women, particularly in regard to those functions that require the exercise of the power of governance or jurisdiction, a power that has traditionally been reserved for those who are ordained. This suggests a separate category of ministry that can be called *jurisdictional ministry*.

The Second Vatican Council clearly taught that lay men and women have a share in the ministerial functions of teaching, sanctifying, and governing (see *Apostolicam Actuositatem*, 2). The Council was ambiguous, however, in its statements on the possibility of laity sharing in the power of governance or jurisdiction, and the final wording of the revised Code retains this ambiguity.

For example, even though lay people are capable of holding ecclesiastical office (c. 228), canon 274 states that only clerics can hold those offices for which the power of orders or governance is required (c. 274.1). Canon 129.1 states that those who have received sacred orders are *habiles* for (that is, capable of possessing and exercising) the power of governance; laity, on the other hand, can "cooperate" in the exercise of that power according to the norms of law (c. 129.2).

The distinction made by the 1983 Code between being capable of possessing and exercising the power of governance as opposed to cooperating in its exercise is new. It is not at all clear what it means to cooperate in the exercise of a power that a person cannot actually hold.

The Church teaches that Christ is the ultimate source of all power in the Church. The basis for participation in the exercise of power is sacramental. The sacraments of Initiation provide the common foundation for all the Christian faithful; for some members of the faithful, the sacrament of Holy Orders provides additional foundation for some functions. Jurisdiction is an additional means to certain functioning, an additional empowerment for certain ministries.

Orders empowers a cleric to perform specific ministerial acts that those without Orders lack the power to perform. Jurisdiction empowers a person to perform certain acts that the Christian without jurisdiction cannot do. Some functions that involve the power of jurisdiction, but that do not require the power of Orders, can be shared with lay persons, and therefore with women, according to canon 129.2. For example, the lay judge on a collegiate court (c. 1421.2); the lay catechist in missionary lands (c. 785); the lay theology teacher (cc. 229.3, 812); the lay witness assisting at marriage (c. 1112); and the lay person preaching (c. 766).

While the 1983 Code recognizes the reality of lay participation in these ministries, the language of the Code is ambiguous when describing the participation of lay men and women in teaching and sanctifying functions that are clearly jurisdictional ministries when exercised by clerics. For example, while priests and deacons are "delegated the faculty" to assist at marriage (c. 1111), the law allows, under certain circumstances, a lay person simply to be "delegated" to do so (c. 1112); no mention of "faculty." While priests and deacons "possess the faculty" to preach everywhere (c. 764), a lay person may be "admitted" to preach in a Church or oratory under certain conditions (c. 766); no mention of "faculty."

Facultas is a word that clearly connotes power. The reluctance of the Code to speak of a *facultas* in regard to the laity exercising these ministries highlights the ambiguity of the Code regarding the lay exercise of the power of governance and jurisdiction. As to the theoretical question, Can lay men and women be empowered to teach, to sanctify, and to govern? it would seem that they are capable of exercising jurisdictional ministries that do not require Holy Orders as a sacramental basis.

In sum, it is clear that lay persons, and therefore women, are permitted to perform several liturgical functions and hold a number of ecclesiastical offices heretofore open only to clergy. However, while we acknowledge the undisputed fact that many more positions in the Church are now open to women than were twenty-five years ago, progress has not kept pace with the official Church's call, in a spirit of co-discipleship, for increased participation of women in church service.

Women, for example, are still prohibited from exercising certain liturgical functions such as assisting at the altar, preaching the homily, and being installed as lectors or acolytes. Women are still barred from holding certain offices in the Church, particularly those that require the exercise of jurisdiction.

Despite the beginnings of progress, there remains a cycle of frustration among women in the Church who want to be genuine partners in ministry; who seek better ways to serve and create a caring community; who want to be judged by their character and competency and not by preconceived notions of their roles; and who want the Church, as an institution and community, to be committed to creating a human environment of collaboration in which the dignity of every person is respected and each baptized believer is called and given a chance to use the gifts God has given to him or to her.

Challenges

This brings me to the third and final part of my comments. At this moment in our experience, what then are some of the challenges that the revised Code raises for the future of women in the mission and ministry of the Church?

Jurisdictional Ministry

The first area that presents a challenge for women in ministry concerns lay participation in jurisdictional ministry. The identification of those functions that require Holy Orders as a sacramental basis for their valid exercise and those that do not is essential if lay men and women are to assume their rightful role in the mission of the Church.

For the future development of the participation of women in ministry, the theoretical question of the laity's "cooperation" in the power of governance becomes a practical concern. Whether it be through consultation or delegation, the more active involvement of lay men and women in the determination of policies that govern Church life at the parish and diocesan levels warrants serious attention.

Implications of addressing this concern might result in lay men and women being given a more active voice in the governance of the Church and a greater recognition of competence, ability, and experience, rather than church status or condition, in appointments to administrative positions in chanceries and parishes. Church leaders are challenged more than ever to enhance the role of the laity, particularly in church governance. This will necessarily mean acknowledging charisms and recognizing competencies, and including lay men and women in decision-making positions at the parish and diocesan levels.

Bill of Rights for Laity

The second area in the revised law that presents a challenge for women in ministry concerns the rights of the Christian faithful as they relate to ministry. The 1917 Code, lacking a theology of the laity, spoke of three fundamental rights proper to the laity: (1) the right to receive the sacraments and participate in worship; (2) the right to associate in associations established by and approved by the hierarchy; and (3) the right to receive adequate religious instruction.

The 1983 Code, on the other hand, presents what some have called a "bill of rights and responsibilities" for all members of the Church in canons 208-231. Specifically, those rights pertaining to the laity only are enumerated in canons 224-231, although canon 224 makes it clear that the rights of the laity are not found exclusively in these eight canons.

Some of the rights recognized in the revised law that have relevance for women in ministry include the right to equality in dignity and activity (c. 208); the right to ecclesiastical office and to assist pastors as experts (c. 228); the right to a theological education (c. 229); the right to academic freedom in the sacred sciences (c. 218); the right to a decent wage (c. 231.2); and the right to juridical protection of one's rights (c. 221).

The participation of lay men and women in the ministry of the Church presupposes and demands a recognition of rights and duties, particularly as they affect those who work for the Church. While every human and ecclesial right proclaimed by the Church is not explicitly mentioned in the 1983 Code, all rights taught by the Magisterium, not only those juridically proclaimed, merit recognition, affirmation, and juridical protection by the Church. It may be necessary, at times, to look beyond the Code for the full picture of human rights recognized and proclaimed by the Church.

In the area of rights, the juridical protection of individual rights presents a challenge for lay men and women in ministry. When the rights of any member have been violated by pastoral action, justice demands—and the Code seeks to guarantee—juridic protection of these rights (c. 221). Concern for the protection of the rights of both administrators and those employed by the Church focuses attention on the policies, structures, and processes that are necessary to provide such protection.

Certain questions arise such as: Do pastoral policies that ensure the just treatment of church personnel exist? Are the structures for protecting the rights of individuals adequate? Can the scope of diocesan tribunals be broadened to adjudicate disputes beyond those involving the nullity of the bond of marriage? Can church officials create alternative means of conflict resolution and grievance redress?

Innovations are needed at the practical level to ensure the protection of rights. Grievance procedures and methods of due process are commendable attempts to meet this need. For rather than creating adversarial situations, they are designed to mediate diverse understandings, alleviate frustrations resulting from human limitations, minimize arbitrariness resulting in real or supposed injustice, and heal painful experiences.

As the number of lay men and women employed in church service expands, the potential for conflict increases. How this conflict is resolved in justice and with equity for all remains an urgent concern and a present challenge.

Preparation for Ministry

The third area of challenge concerns the issue of adequate preparation, required by canon 231.1, of lay men and women who devote themselves to special service in the Church. The explosion of ministries within the Church since Vatican II has brought with it accompanying concerns about appropriate formation and preparation of those who minister. Up to now, most resources for preparation of persons involved in church service have been concentrated in seminaries and novitiates, with few resources being allocated for the preparation of lay men and women. If the institutions providing the training are closed to them, lay men and women cannot obtain the necessary preparation. Policies of admission to formation programs may have to be changed if alternative training possibilities are not provided in dioceses.

In recent years, some dioceses have consolidated resources and developed ministry-formation programs that include permanent deacons and lay men and women preparing for church ministry. Whatever model for training is adopted, it is clear that if women are to participate more actively in church ministry, the Church will have to be prepared to provide them with adequate preparation.

Closely related to the issue of ministry formation and preparation is the right of the lay person employed in church service to receive a just wage and appropriate benefits (c. 231,2). Recognition of this right challenges church leaders to develop comprehensive personnel systems based on principles of justice that apply to all employed in church service. In such a system, the primary focus is on the equitable treatment of all employees rather than on the development of separate systems for clergy, religious, and laity.

Conclusion

In conclusion, let me simply say that the issues and challenges associated with the changing role of women in the Code and in the Church ought to be viewed in the context of the developing role of the laity in the Church. The 1983 Code, as we have seen, presents several challenges for the development of ministry and for the participation of women in that ministry. How can we begin to meet them? Basic to any response is collaboration and cooperation. All of us—women and men, lay, clergy, and religious—are called to devise creative and reasoned responses to present-day church experience.

The implications of the revised law for the participation of women in the ministry of the Church will not be resolved on the basis of theory alone. It is at the level of experience and *praxis*, in light of the needs and resources of each local Church, that such questions and concerns will be worked out as well.

Reflection Questions

1. Sr. Sharon Euart, RSM, refers to a "bill of rights and responsibilities" in the revised 1983 *Code of Canon Law*. What advantage does this bill of rights give women? What practical applications does it have for women in the Church today?

2. Canon 231.1 of the Code requires adequate preparation of lay persons who devote themselves to special service in the Church. Since many institutes of training are closed to lay men and women, how can people at the diocesan and parish levels reformulate policies and programs to ensure the needed training of lay men and women who wish to participate in church ministry?

Workshop Model 2
Pro-Life and Feminist?
Helen Alvaré

A pro-life position is a true feminist position for a variety of reasons. Beginning in the Christian tradition, we notice that the Bible speaks not only of freedom *from* burdens, but also of freedom *for* responsibility. Bringing new life into the world and rearing that child require a decision to be free for that responsibility and for the life of that child.

Christian Tradition and Freedom

Although St. Paul speaks often of freedom in his epistles, he concludes that love triumphs over freedom. In the name of love for others, one's own freedom should be curtailed. Love for the new human being created at conception must triumph over a desire for freedom of another sort.

Pro-Life and Feminist? Helen Alvaré, director of planning and information, NCCB Secretariat for Pro-Life Activities, addresses a workshop on feminism from a pro-life perspective.

St. Augustine discusses the difference between free choice and freedom. *Free choice* involves arbitrary decisions to choose one thing and not another, at discrete moments and time. *Freedom* is the desire to want to do the good thing. A pro-life stance encourages *real* freedom, not mere free choice to dispose of or keep developing new life.

A legitimate critique of these Christian sources notes that women often are called upon to subjugate their freedom for others. The pro-life response does not "throw out the baby with the bath water" by disregarding the value to the Christian of freedom. Rather, it asks men to help in the work of freedom, to undertake freedom *for* responsibility. In addition, a pro-life position recognizes the integrity of women, including their ability to bear children. It recommends social policy that treats women in their real state, which often involves them as mothers and caretakers. Pro-life recognizes the critical importance of relationships. In feminist thinking, relationships and women's valuing of relationships have great importance. The pro-life position does not ask women to break off a vital relationship with their unborn child in the name of another good.

Pro-life feminism sees women's dilemmas in crisis pregnancies as part of society's dilemma. It makes a pregnant woman part of society's community of care and asks society to develop and sustain social policies that address the reasons why women might be driven to abortion and the incentives that would allow more women to bear and keep their children. Pro-life feminism does not ask women to attain their freedom by sacrificing another's life. It treats women not as victims but as responsible adults.

Abortion Advocacy Is Not Feminist

- *Abortion is a violent act.* Feminists encourage resolution of problems by nonviolent solutions.

- *Abortion advocacy allows society to treat women as if their ability to bear children is superfluous or burdensome.* It is a cheap short-term solution that allows society to avoid long-term responsibility for the life it creates. It encourages society to formulate policy that does not take women's child-bearing role into consideration.

- *Men support abortion in greater numbers than women.* Is this a way of making women more sexually available to men?

- *Because of the way society has structured legalized abortion, women often are isolated to make their decision without the advice and counsel of husband or parents.* Women are excluded from the community of care and told to make this decision as if it were not the ones requiring care and advice.

Reflection Questions

1. How would Helen Alvaré define true Christian feminism? How does this definition differ from the way some feminists define the term?

2. What does real freedom mean to someone who takes a a pro-life position?

3. In our parishes and communities, how can we help women to appreciate what freedom means when they are burdened by poverty or discrimination because of their minority status?

Workshop Model 3
What Is Women's Unique Spirituality?
Dana Greene

Framing the Discussion

Defining spirituality is like attempting to nail jellyfish to the wall. But, generally speaking, spirituality is concerned with how we can live in such a way as to love God and others. In our discussion today, we are equal resources to each other. Each of us approaches spirituality from our own unique experience, experience that may help others. Spiritual writer Evelyn Underhill said that the spiritual life is simply one lived from the center, where we are anchored in God. Our question then is twofold: How do we get there? and What keeps us there?

Who Are We?

Spirituality is always colored by our own culture. We are women living in the late-twentieth century in the United States. On the verge of a new century, we live in a violent world, yet a world where boredom is a problem for many people. Finding reason for hope is a problem for many others.

A British bishop in the African Sudan tells the story of the hopelessness caused by starvation, a starvation caused mainly by humankind's inhumanity. The bishop tells of a mother who sees her children's bellies grow large from starvation. Having no food, one day she gathers stones and puts them in a pot with water and puts it on to boil. Then she tells her children to go outside and play, and they go, filled with a sense of hope that supper will come. Meanwhile, the mother goes out to the brush looking for a bone to finish the meal and, indeed, finds something to make the soup nourishing.

The point of the stone soup story is that hope forces us to look in out-of-the-way places. If we live in a culture of hopelessness, one source of hope for Christians comes from the knowledge that God has loved us.

Prayer: The Key to Hope

Prayer helps us see differently. The mystic Simone Weil wrote that prayer is the opportunity to be won over by God. Evelyn Underhill said that prayer allows us to stand beside the Artist-Lover: God. Prayer is the cauldron that refines us and makes us prophets in the world and in the Church.

I read the Book of Wisdom in preparing these remarks. Wisdom passes into holy people from age to age. Wisdom makes us friends of God and the prophets. What is it to be Catholic today and a friend of God? Prayer is a means of being intimate with God. Prayer is the mandate of every Christian. Prayer makes us docile to God. But prayer also gives us courage and makes us freer to love others. Prayer is a methodology—a way of becoming.

The poet T. S. Eliot said that there are times when the best people lack conviction and the worst are filled with passion and intensity. Our passion can be muted by the complexity of our world. But through prayer, we can rekindle our hope and our passion.

Hunches about Women's Spirituality

- Women's spirituality is not a monastic spirituality, a retreat from the world, a way of leaving the brokenness of our world.

- Women need to take a vastly more important role in shaping their own spirituality. The Judaic-Christian spiritual tradition was shaped by men for men. Women are added on to this tradition.

- Women through nature and nurture weave together a wholeness that integrates and blesses and brings hope out of ambiguity. This ability of women helps during hopeless times—when they face the disarray of families, the specter of war, the failure of religious institutions. During such times, prayer is invaluable. You have to have hope that God lives in the midst of such times. Prayer helps align us with the good.

Jesus said, "I have come that you may have life"—which implies hope. How to begin: Gather what we have: a stone, a pot, and water.

Reflection Questions

1. What do you think it means to be a twentieth-century Catholic woman and a friend of God? How can women be spiritual resources for one another?

2. Where in your daily life do you find time to pray? Do you prefer to pray alone or with others? Why?

3. Considering your own individual life-style, what contributions do you make to women's spirituality in your parish or community?

Workshop Model 4
Women and Aging: An Outline

I. Opening (10 minutes)

Welcome everyone to the workshop. Begin by having each person briefly introduce himself or herself to the group. Next, explain the purpose of workshop as well as the desired outcome. For example: It is a forum where participants can share their experiences on the topic and exchange ideas and methods of how they are addressing the issue of women and aging at the diocesan and local levels.

II. Who Is the Older Woman? (20 minutes)

A. What Women Say about Growing Older

Set the scene by reading a pertinent quote from an older woman of your choice. For example, the Jungian psychologist Florida Scott-Maxwell, who wrote the following in a journal called *The Measure of My Days* (New York: Penguin, 1968), pp. 5 and 13:

> We who are old know that age is more than a disability. It is an intense and varied experience, almost beyond our capacity at times, but something to be carried high. If it is a long defeat, it is also a victory....

> Age puzzles me. I thought it was a quiet time. My 70s were interesting and fairly serene, but my 80s are passionate. I grow more intense as I age. To my own surprise, I burst out with hot conviction. Only a few years ago I enjoyed my tranquility; now I am so disturbed by the outer world and by human quality in general that I want to put things right, as though I still owed a debt to life.

B. Statistics on Women as They Age

Handouts are good wherever possible. The American Association of Retired Persons (AARP) offers good materials on the subject of older women for little or no cost (an advantage for church groups with budget problems.) An AARP pamphlet entitled *Why* points out the following:

- More than 80% of the nearly 9 million Americans aged sixty-five and older and living alone are women.

- Women make up 59% of those aged sixty-five or older, but they comprise 72% of the elderly poor.

- One in four women who live to be eighty-five will spend some time in a nursing home.

In 1986, the New York State Catholic Conference's Commission on the Elderly published the following statistics:

- Two-thirds of all people now alive in the United States will live into their eighties.

- By 2015, one of every six people will be over sixty-five.

- Women aged sixty-five and older now outnumber men of the same age by three to two.

C. Our Responsibility toward Women as They Age

What we have said so far indicates that the topic of women and aging is an important one for the Church. If the general population in the United States is aging, our parish congregations also are aging. This offers us both a challenge and an opportunity:

- *Challenge:* To discover how to help older women find satisfying ways to structure their lives and to navigate the highs and lows of aging.

- *Opportunity:* Once people retire, they often have an amazing amount of time, energy, and resources that might be channeled productively into service within the Church and within their local communities.

III. Small-Group Discussion (45 minutes)

If the group contains fewer than ten people, do not break into smaller groups; however, if there are more than ten people, have them break into groups of six to eight so that each person can be heard. Choose a group leader, who will guide the discussion, and a recorder, who will make a brief report back to the larger group. The following questions might be used to focus discussion:

- What are some of the stereotypes of the elderly that affect how we view and approach older people as individuals? What can we do to alter or eliminate these stereotypes?

- From your personal experience, what would you consider to be the primary needs of women as they age? Why?

- As a parish or diocesan community, what can we do to help older women?

- As a Church, how can we best utilize the experience and wisdom of older women in our parishes and dioceses?

IV. Wrap-Up (15 minutes)

At this time, the small groups reassemble into one group. Have each of the recorders give a brief report on his or her group's discussion. Using newsprint sheets or large poster boards, write down pertinent points arising from the individual discussions. Then, give the participants an opportunity to briefly discuss these points. Before dismissing the participants, hand out a resource list (sample follows).

Sample Resource List on Aging

Bianchi, Eugene. *Aging as a Spiritual Journey*. New York: Crossroad Publishers, 1982.

Bird, Caroline. *The Good Years: Your Life in the Twenty-First Century*. New York: E. P. Dutton, 1983.

Deedy, John. *Your Aging Parents*. Chicago: Thomas More Press, 1984.

Fischer, Edward. *Life in the Afternoon: Good Ways of Growing Older*. Mahwah, N.J.: Paulist Press, 1987.

Meyer, Charles. *Surviving Death: A Practical Guide to Caring for the Dying and Bereaved*. Mystic, Conn.: Twenty-Third Publications, 1988.

Morrison, Ruth and Dawn Radtke. *Aging with Joy*. Mystic, Conn.: Twenty-Third Publications, 1988.

Sarton, May. *At Seventy*. New York: W. N. Norton Co., 1984.

Silverstone, Barbara and Helen Kandel Hyman. *You and Your Aging Parent: The Modern Family's Guide to Emotional, Physical and Financial Problems*. New York: Pantheon, 1982.

Other Topics for Workshop Development

The following are suggested topics for workshop development. Use one or more of them to design an individually tailored workshop for your local diocese or parish community. Or create your own topic, which reflects a specific area of interest or a pertinent diocesan/parish issue.

Women as Care-Givers: Their Many Faces. Women face many difficult situations in their roles as care-givers (e.g., families struggling with AIDS, divorce, drugs, and poverty; single-parent families; caring for aged or disabled family members). What can we, as Church, do to help women cope with the demands of these roles? What programs or support structures are available in your local community? in your diocesan community?

Single Mothers: Stresses and Growths. What are some of the supports and sources of strength that we, as Church, can offer to single mothers? What does spirituality have to say to single parents? What is faith's role in helping these busy women cope with their difficult responsibilities?

Women and the Arts. Women who choose to pursue a career in the arts face many difficulties, given their other pressing responsibilities. What are their strengths? their needs? How can we, as Church, help them to achieve a balance in their lives?

Men and Women Collaborating in the Mission of the Church. What are some of the areas in which men and women practice team ministry? What are some of the advantages of collaborative ministry? some of the stresses and pitfalls?

Sisterhood: Reaching Out to Immigrants. As Church, what responsibilities do we have to make immigrants feel at home in our midst? What issues affect immigrants today? How can the new immigrants enrich us? What contributions and gifts do they bring to the Church?

Single Women in the Church and in Society. Single women comprise a noticeable part of any parish, particularly when the increasing number of older women are taken into account. What are some of the unique needs and concerns of single women? How can the Church make an effort to include them in its worship life? in its institutional life?

Sexism and Racism as Factors in the Feminization of Poverty. The increasing burden of poverty in the United States today is borne in disproportionate numbers by women and children. What is meant by the term "feminization of poverty"? How does society perpetuate certain injustices that contribute to the oppression of women? What can the Church do to ensure "economic justice for all"?

Language and Other Symbols of Equality. Many women in the Church today express feelings of exclusion, be it in worship or in certain administrative areas. What role does language play in fostering these feelings? What are some of the other traditional symbols that have served to perpetuate this "exclusion"? What can be done to make women feel that they share equally in the life of the Church?

Inclusive Family Ministry. There are many dimensions of family ministry in today's complex society. What programs are available in your diocesan or parish community that deal with ministry to divorced and separated Catholics? marriage preparation and enrichment? ministry to children? counseling? peer ministry? natural family planning? If no program or support group currently exists to deal with a specific aspect of family ministry, what can you do to help establish such a program?

Women Administrators of Priestless Parishes. What happens when "father" is actually a lay woman, a nun, or a deacon? This topic addresses how parishioners in some parishes without resident priests have had to adjust to women administrators. In what ways might such an administration differ from a more traditional male-dominated administration? How do you think you would react to a woman administrator? Why? What are some of the unique problems and issues facing women in church administration today? Research indicates that "female" ministry style tends to be "collaborative;" why do you think this might be?

Baptismal Equality: Issues in Seminary Formation. How can involving seminarians in parish and educational situations where they encounter both men and women help them later on in their ministry? How do these parish and/or educational situations help to make seminarians more aware of the issues of equality? Why is this awareness so important in and for the Church today? What can we do to foster this interaction among seminarians and men and women on the diocesan and/or parish level?

Spiritual Exercises

Spirituality and prayer play a significant part in any gathering of God's people. So it was at The Wisdom of Women Symposium. Daily sessions began with, and often ended with, prayer. Participants prayed alone and with others. To encourage private prayer and reflection, a room was set aside for meditation; its decor evoked a peaceful, spiritual atmosphere. One prayer session combined the elements of piano and song, featuring two talented musicians, Isabella Bates and Nora Gibson. Still other prayer sessions were planned and led by women's groups from around the country.

In this section, two models are provided to help guide you in developing the spiritual component of your workshop. The Morning Prayer Service, prepared by women from the Diocese of Saginaw, includes a water ceremony, which reminds us of our need to be washed clean. The Concluding Prayer Service, prepared by the National Council of Catholic Women, features candles lit in ceremony and passed from one person to the other, which reminds us how we are called to be light to one another.

Note: When planning any prayer service or community program in which music and/or songs are to be photocopied and distributed to the participants, permission must be obtained from the copyright holders of the music in question. Whenever possible, use hymnals or missalettes.

Morning Prayer Service
Prepared by the Diocese of Saginaw

(The service requires a leader and a music minister.)

Opening Prayer

Leader:
Holy God, fill us this day with new breath.
All:
And we shall be living words of praise.

Song: "Song of the Body of Christ" by David Haas (or another song appropriate to your particular needs and the theme of your event)

The Magnificat: Luke 1:47-55

Scripture Reading: Matthew 15:21-28

Personal Reflection

Each person meditates silently.
Or:
One person gives a personal meditation based on the theme of the workshop, symposium, or conference.

Prayers of Petition

(These should be based on your parish or diocesan situation and the theme chosen for your workshop, symposium, or conference.)
Response: Lord, hear our prayer.

Raise Your Voices in Song. Participants join together in song during one of the symposium's prayer services.

<u>*Water Ritual:*</u>   Galatians 3:26-29 (read aloud)

(This ceremony includes a ritual dipping of hands in a basin of water. Depending on number of people involved, have at least two people holding basins of water for participants.)

<u>*Concluding Song:*</u>   "Song of the Body of Christ"

Concluding Prayer Service
Prepared by the National Council of Catholic Women

(The service requires a leader and a music minister.)

Greeting

Leader:
To our God who shares divinity with us.
To our God who shares humanity with us.
To our God who unsettles and inspires us.

All:
Let us give praise and thanks. Amen.

Song:
"O How I Long to See" by Bob Hurd (or another song appropriate to your particular needs and the theme of your event)

Prayer:
"The Wisdom of Hope" (read by alternate sides)

Left Side:
O God of all the universe, we praise and thank you for all the good gifts that you have given us, and especially for the gift of light to see with hope-filled eyes.

Right Side:
We ask that you will renew our sight, so that we may envision a new heaven and a new earth; a world in which all women and men will work together joyfully in cooperation and love.

Left Side:
These are new and challenging times in the Church and in the world. Give us wisdom so that we may be always conscious of tradition yet open to the new ways in which the Spirit calls us.

Right Side:
Guide us as we share the wisdom that we have found in

this gathering in a manner that does not confine or limit others. Give us a spirit of trust so that we may more fully collaborate with each other.

Left Side:
May our lives be those of a priestly people; a people who are filled with hope because of your presence in our midst; a people who recognize that it is in serving our sisters and brothers that we serve you.

Right Side:
We ask you all these favors because you are the giver of life and light, the One who enlightens our vision, touches it with wisdom, and gives it strength and brilliance.

<u>Psalmody:</u> Psalm 126

<u>Scripture Reading:</u> Wisdom 7:24-29

<u>Litany of Hope</u>

(After the leader reads the entire line, the assembly repeats the part in italics.)

Blessed be Eve, the first woman in our tradition, whose very life gives us a lesson in hope for the future of humanity.

Blessed be Sarah, partner of Abraham, whose ability to remain open to laughter, love, and the miracle of creation gave her a son in her old age.

Blessed be Mary, the Mother of God and our Mother, who knew pain and humiliation, yet never lost faith.

Blessed be Prisca, collaborator with Paul, whose faith and hope enabled him to minister.

Blessed be Teresa of Avila, doctor of the Church, whose experience of the awareness of God teaches all generations the value of prayer in times of doubt.

Blessed be Dorothy Day, cofounder of the Catholic Worker Movement, who has given hope and witness to the Church of the poor and the oppressed.

Blessed be women religious, vowed celibates, who have served the Church tirelessly through all the ages and have never lost faith.

Blessed be single women, mothers to many, who by their unique call offer time and talents to all God's family.

Blessed be wives and mothers, who have nurtured children and families in a spirit of joy, hope, and self-giving.

Blessed be widows, who in sorrow and loss are signs of fidelity, perseverance, and strength.

Blessed be poor women and women who are abused or oppressed, for they give to all of us a lesson of determination and hope.

Prayer

> Leader:
> Creator God, You who have given us these strong yet gentle women, help us to draw strength from their lives so that we may be ever faithful. We ask this through Christ our Lord. Amen.

Candle Ceremony

> (Distribute candles. Then, using the flame from candles on the altar, pass the light from one person to the next until all candles are lighted. Hold lighted candles during the following song.)

<u>Meditation Song:</u>   "St. Theresa's Prayer" by John Michael Talbot

Final Blessing

<u>Closing Song:</u>   "City of God" by Dan Schutte

Wrap-Up

When designing a workshop, a symposium, or a conference on women's issues, it is important to allocate enough time at the end for a summation of what has occurred during the gathering and to offer some ideas on where the next steps might lead. Providing participants with an opportunity to speak is a vital part of any summation. An Open Forum, in which women and men are invited to come together to discuss women's issues, is an ideal way to conclude your workshop, symposium, or conference. The summation period is to give participants an opportunity to express publicly their views and to let them know that they were listened to with respect. The excerpts presented here are meant to guide you as you design and develop your own Open Forum. You are invited to build on and to improve this model, structuring it to suit your own needs.

This Wrap-Up section provides excerpts from the concluding session of The Wisdom of Women Symposium, which was comprised of three interrelated parts:

1. ***A Summary.*** After listening carefully, taking copious notes, and reflecting on what she had seen and heard, Susan Muto summarized the symposium for participants in "Framing a Call to Action." Ms. Muto is a noted writer and speaker in the field of spirituality, currently living in Pittsburgh, Pennsylvania. She has served as staff and chief writer to the U.S. bishops' committee established to prepare the pastoral on women.

2. ***A Vision for the Future.*** Bishop Joseph Imesch, of Joliet, Illinois, followed Ms. Muto's summary with a reflection on the proposed pastoral on women. Bishop Imesch is chairman of the NCCB Writing Committee for the Pastoral on Women and past chairman of the NCCB Committee on Women in Society and in the Church.

3. ***Voices of Women.*** Concluding this section is a brief selection of views from women symposium participants. These anonymous "Voices" represent a wide variety of backgrounds, life-styles, and interests. They emerged from the small-group discussions that were held during the concluding session and from individual points of view raised during the symposium.

Framing a Call to Action
Susan Muto

Symbols are important in our life and in our personal spirituality. Behind me are banners, and in the middle of those banners is a wreath symbolizing the season, Advent, but it is also a symbol of welcome. I ask you now to place yourselves imaginatively within that circle; to know that we are one or two gathered in Jesus's name, that Jesus is with us; to experience amidst the beauty, the grace, the astounding delight of diversity in this room, our unity in that circle of welcome. We are young, middle-aged, and old. We are women representing a rich, multicultural diversity. In this room with us, spiritually, are spouses and children, aunts, uncles, grandparents, and all of us brought together in that circle of welcome. Let us stand there as we try to summarize and draw together what we have been doing.

Poetry does it better than prose, and I will begin by sharing with you an excerpt from a beautiful poem by Jessica Powers, Sister of Miriam of the Holy Spirit, *The Will of God*:

> Time has one song alone. If you are heedful
> and concentrate on song with all your soul,
> you may hear the song of the beautiful will of God,
> soft notes or deep sonorous tones that roll
> like thunder over time.
> Not many have the hearing for this music
> and fewer still have sought it as sublime.
>
> Listen, and tell your grief: God is singing!
> God sings through all creation with His will.
> Save the negation of sin, all is His music, . . .
> The saints who loved have died of this pure music,
> and no one enters heaven till he learns,
> deep in his soul, at least, to sing with God.

In thinking how to summarize this symposium, it occurred to me that now is not the time to reiterate the issues that are so important to us in a point-counterpoint fashion. You know what they are. They have been named for us in seminars and in plenary sessions. You know and I know that we have got to go home and do our homework.

We have to begin with prayer. Always begin with prayer. We must raise all of these issues to a transcendent plane where we can understand the wider issue and the wider vision. And, in that light, in the light of the treasure, Scripture, and our teaching tradition, to carry on with study and action as necessary and as we are called forth by the Spirit.

And all of us must be faithful to our call. In the long run, it is on that we will be judged. Some are called to silent contemplative prayer. Some are called to write poetry. Some are called to stand on the forefront and dare to tell it like it is in no uncertain terms, and to keep knocking on that door until that door made of iron melts as soft wax.

What is our call? And, how can we carry that forth? That is for us to decide. What recommendations to make to your diocese, to your bishops, that is what you will determine. It depends on you. It depends on your responding to the grace rolling through you that has drawn you here and will draw you forth.

These are some thoughts that I had by way of targeting what we had in common and those great streams of wisdom and insight that have circulated through this room with all of the immense and beautiful diversity that has surrounded it. I have five points to make.

1. A Narrative Spirituality

We have risked to dive into the waters of what I like to call the *deep feminine*, which courses also through the veins of the masculine as well; the deep feminine that is associated with the knowledge of the heart. Assembled in this room are men and women of high intelligence, representing the incredible fields of law, teaching, medicine, the arts; they also represent that beautiful and most important vocation of homemaking and mothering.

We have been astounded by the knowledge of the heart, which has taken those words and taken that intelligence and risked to hook it in to life experience so that what has been said has emerged out of reality, has emerged in dialogue with life experience. This plunging, this diving into the deep feminine, will always emerge in the form of a narrative spirituality—a spirituality that is experiential and numinous, that is balanced and witty and wise, that is silent and outspoken.

We have heard it said, "Trust your story." Thank God for your experience of joy and sorrow, of elation and pain, because it is out of this story that we will be in touch more and more with the truth of what God is asking of us.

2. Conversion

A keynote that never ceases to rumble and resonate as we listen, a keynote that was vitally important in both drafts of the pastoral document on women, is conversion of heart. This call to conversion has been issued again and again, at table and in assemblies. Conversion is an ongoing issue, recognizing that all of us can become inordinately attached to plans, to projects, to committee meetings, to the whole functional model.

We have to press the boundaries where people begin to acknowledge there is that of us which is still out of step and which must submit itself to the *metanoia*, to the grace, which alone can reform and save us deep down inside.

We met converted hearts this week. We met people who have transcended fear and who have been launched by God on the wings of freedom, free from inordinate attachment to power and pleasure and possession, free on the wings of grace to tell it from the depths and to hope that God will use that as God will.

3. Partnership

In so many instances, we heard a call for a new sensitivity to formation in mutuality, partnership, and friendship. It has been wonderful to watch people socialize together, put their arms around one another, hug, shake hands, exchange peace. We have seen modeled for us on panels, mutuality, friendship, and partnership. Whatever else you take back from this symposium, take back this conviction that formation and mutuality, partnership and friendship are of God.

I have said to my own family, when I travel again to yet another pastoral writing committee meeting, I am going to spend some days with people who have become good and treasured friends, and we are going to try again to do the best we can to listen and to reflect and to respond. We have had some great times and some difficult times, but it has all been worth it.

4. Systemic Change

I want us to be aware that systemic change of structures begins with inner conversion. To bear fruit, we have to be willing to let that fruit-bearing tree take root deeply in an interior awareness that, without God, we are and can do nothing; but with God, we may be called to stretch and to move into places where we never would have imagined ourselves going.

Systemic change can only happen in dialogue with the treasures of our faith tradition in openness to the grace of God's call through prayer, study and reflection, and continual self-examination.

Our pride can and does get in the way. That cultural pressure for instant change tomorrow can incline us to overlook the nuances that are precious and important. What I am saying here is that our desire, our call, to change what can be changed must begin with inner change. We have to change as people.

We are all part of these oppressive structures, and we have to begin again through prayer and self-examination to find those simple pockets in ourselves where change has to occur. But, I think we have to do it without losing laughter. We have to do it without losing compassion for the vulnerability of our own and others' human condition.

There you have it: knowledge of the heart; conversion of heart; formation in mutuality; wise, systemic change in dialogue with inner personal change.

5. Spiritual Underpinnings

Some of the most precious memories that I will take home with me have been our prayer and eucharistic services. I talked with women who went back to their rooms and wept for singing together in a room of over 300 some of the songs that we love so well, for the magnificent power of our gospel choir and the gathering together of all around the circle of love and peace that is the Eucharist.

I love this Catholic Church to which I belong. Sometimes, I envision it as a great ship in the middle of an ocean way down in the depths, thrusting, and there may be some big holes. And somebody says, "Quick, get a lifeboat. It's sinking." And I think about that and I say, "Give me a pail. I'm going to go down in this storm bailing, because I'm not getting off this ship."

This is the ship of my peasant Italian grandmother who was shipped over from Italy into an arranged marriage. She had eleven children, five of whom died of various diseases. I only knew her until I was twelve years old, but she remains for me a living, breathing pillar of peasant faith.

I believe that we have had an opportunity here to reclaim the foundations of our faith tradition—to go back and stand through the story that people told of their teachers—and to remember that it is on the ground of that incredible overwhelming conviction that is faith, that becomes hope, that becomes love, that makes all of this struggle worthwhile.

We are only in the first 2,000 years of Christianity. Two thousand years from now, people will look back on the primitive Church of the first 2,000 years and understand how, with all the goodwill in the world, we messed it up but good. We are beginning to understand what it means "to love one another as I have loved you." We have all seen the horror of what happens when that commandment is not adhered to, so we stand on the ground of a powerful faith tradition.

Whatever else has happened for you these days, leave here satisfied and elated and full of hope. God is with us. God will not leave us orphans. God enjoys what we are doing here. God likes the fact that we are not going to give up.

A Vision for the Future
Bishop Joseph Imesch

Bishop Clark began this symposium by talking about conversion. Somewhere along the line, he also talked about "a pilgrim people." I love that image of being on pilgrimage. You have all been on a tour; you know what that is like. It is very difficult to keep the group together. There is always someone who is late, always someone who is lost, always someone who wants to go on ahead.

I say that to you, and to myself, because we are on a pilgrimage and there are people who are running way ahead, and there are people who are lagging way behind, and there are some who are going off on side streets. Somehow, we have to keep the group together. We cannot let those who are running ahead be so far ahead of us that we lose sight of them, or lose sight of those who are having difficulty keeping up with us. We are "a pilgrim people," but we are also a community—God's chosen people. So I just pray that we stay together, that we allow some to run ahead, and that we allow some to stay behind, but that we never allow either group to get so far apart that we forget we are a people.

That said, I want to talk to you this morning about the pastoral on women and to tell you that it is alive and well. It may be on life support systems, but it is alive; the plug has not been pulled. The doctors have said, "Yes, there is still light; we see some movement; let us see if we can save it."

At the last bishops' meeting, the bishops voted to continue the process of the pastoral. Our committee is very grateful for that. We are unanimous in our feeling that this pastoral letter has to go forward. This is not a time—after seven years—to say, "We have nothing to say to women." Bishops have not spoken to women in any way except by their silence. However, the last bishops' meeting did produce one very positive effort in inclusive language in Scripture; a mere baby step, but a step. Our committee feels very strongly that it is because of the pastoral letter on women that this is happening. Also because of the pastoral letter, women's commissions are being established in many places; this was unheard of seven years ago.

I think that the bishops are very sensitive to the concerns of women. I sense that from bishops who come and tell me: "I never realized the depth of feeling on the part of the women in the Church." Women had never been asked what they thought or what they felt before. The response from women was good, even though it was difficult for us to hear. We have to hear it, and you have to make it possible for us to hear it. You have to speak up and let us know so that we can be aware of your concerns and your needs.

One of the things that caused a delay in the vote on the pastoral letter in November 1990 was a letter from the pope's secretary of state to Archbishop Pilarczyk, suggesting that it would be good if this topic could be discussed with members of other national hierarchies. I cannot quote the exact sentence, but there was a sentence that said something like, "The Holy Father feels this is a topic of such interest that it needs to be discussed at a greater level." We are very grateful for that. We are happy for that opportunity to meet with members of other national hierarchies to discuss the concerns of women.

At our meeting in Washington, the bishops also stated very clearly that they need to discuss this letter among themselves; they need to feel that they own this letter in a way that they still have not achieved. And so, I have asked that a two- to three-hour period be allocated during an upcoming bishops' meeting for discussion of the pastoral. Then, God willing, in either June 1992 or, at the latest, November 1992, we will have a final draft that will be presented to the bishops for their vote.

This pastoral letter is not the final word. No one says final words, only God. We expect this to be a beginning. We feel that without this pastoral letter, what is happening here will not continue. We feel that we need a basis for discussion, and the pastoral allows that. It covers all kinds of issues that are of concern to women, and it puts the bishops on the line as saying something specific about those concerns.

We need your support and your help; we need you to tell your own bishop that this is something of importance, a great deal of importance. This pastoral is the product of what you and 100,000 other women have said; that has never happened before. The pastoral has limitations; it is not able to say everything. It is written for a particular country; it is not a universal document. But, although it speaks to the people of our country, it has to be in communion with the universal Church.

Basically, that is where the the pastoral letter is at this point in the process. I thank ail of you for your patient endurance. It is a lifelong—and perhaps, more than a lifelong—task. I do believe, however, the Lord is with us; we are his chosen people. I believe in the Spirit guiding the Church; I believe that with every fiber in me. No matter what it might look like, no matter what happens, the Spirit is with the Church. Bless you.

Voices of Women

An ideal way to conclude your workshop, symposium, or conference is to schedule an Open Forum, which encourages maximum participation of those attending the event. Not only does this type of forum offer participants an opportunity to voice their deep-felt concerns about the various issues raised during the sessions, but it also allows them to feel that they have been listened to—and heard. Though different points of view may exist, the act of listening becomes an exercise in understanding other people and their perspectives.

How to proceed:

- Place microphones near the front on both sides of the auditorium or meeting room. If you have a large group, you may wish to place microphones near the middle of the room as well.

- Have a moderator guide the questions and facilitate the flow of the discussion so that all participants who wish to contribute are afforded the opportunity.

- Have the moderator explain the ground rules before the forum begins (e.g., five minutes per speaker; show respect for each person's point of view; only one speaker at a time).

Some of the many "voices" of women who attended the symposium are heard in the following brief comments, which also reflect the diversity in our Church today. Each heading indicates a separate "voice."

Education. As a high school graduate, a gardener, and a housekeeper, I feel that the average Catholic woman has not been represented here. Yesterday, in discussing the formation of women's committees within each parish and diocese, it was suggested that the committee panels be comprised of women who were educated at the college level. Please do not make the mistake of leaving out those of us who have less education. Just because I do not have a college degree and fifteen letters behind my name, that does not mean that I do not know anything.

Raising Consciousness on Women's Issues. We feel that the bishops who are with us today should go and talk with the bishops throughout the United States and sensitize them more to the concerns of women in the community. We also feel that we need to mobilize, at the local level, with the ministry of listening and truly voice the concerns of the women in the pew.

Minority Representation. We have heard here of the oppression of women in the Church. Well, I feel doubly oppressed as a woman and as a Hispanic. I am here because I share many of your same concerns regarding the active participation of women in the ministry of the Church. We have heard it said here that women are denied full authority in the Church. This is also true for lay men and for priests. The Church is not a democracy. Jesus never took votes, nor did he ask for any input when he established the Church. Some of us love our Church as it is. To conclude, let me just say that in 1979, Pope John Paul II, speaking to a group of religious women, during a visit to the United States, said to them that they have been baptized into the priesthood of Jesus Christ. What more can we ask?

Voicing Concern. One of the symposium's participants, Jo Ann Harvey, joins in a discussion of women's concerns.

Domestic Violence. One area that has not had an appropriate forum this weekend is the issue of domestic violence, including child and spousal abuse as well as neglect. The alternative is the creation of healthy individuals and healthy family systems. I promised the children and the women that I see on a daily basis that I would be a voice for them and that I would not allow their concerns to go unheard. Often, those who are experiencing domestic violence are so entrenched in their lives that they do not have a voice with which to speak. Speaking up demands a knowledge of self-worth, but continual abuse and violence suffocate the voice of the victim by demeaning and destroying the human spirit. I truly believe that the voice of the Church must ring out concretely for the women and children who suffer, until all of us can be liberated from a system that is oppressively violent and live side by side with one another. As you continue your work on the pastoral, I urge you to work intensely and vigorously in this area. A profound and moving statement needs to be made about changing our system so that violence can be eradicated. I also urge that this message find its way to the pulpit, and thereby to the entire Church, not just through the words of the pastoral, but also through the words of those who preach to the people in the pews.

Value of the Symposium. I cannot begin to describe to you how, for the most part, this whole gathering has been so positive for me. It has been wonderful. I would like to say a few words on behalf of the women who are not represented here because their diocese did not send delegates to this symposium. Let us find a way to locate the women who would want to be here, who would benefit as we all have benefited, and let us get them here. If we are "a pilgrim people," as Bishop Imesch said, some of us lag behind, and some of us get lost. I think these women are lost, through no fault of their own. Let us find them; let us meet again; and let us move forward together.

More Effective Communication. We want to tell the [bishops' pastoral] writing committee that a lot of people are not getting any information about what is being done. We also want to say thank you for this conference; we would like to have another one in the future. Personally, I would like to say that what I heard articulated this morning by the women in the various ethnic groups was truly powerful. I am proud to be part of a Church where the women can speak so well. Thank you for that.

Children and Their Needs. I do not know if there is any greater cause that women can and should identify with than that of children and adolescents who are suffering throughout the world, particularly here in this country. As women of the Church, I think we should make a commitment to do everything in our power to safeguard the future for our children. To that end, whatever is possible to do on the national, diocesan, or parish level to further the cause of children and adolescents, please, let us see to it that it is done.

Reflection Questions

1. What does Susan Muto mean by the "deep feminine"? How is this reflected in the symposium? Why does she feel that systemic change is necessary? Do you agree with her? Why?

2. The Catholic Church in the United States embraces many different points of view. How can a symposium on women's issues help to bring about a greater understanding—and perhaps, even conversion—to its participants?

3. If you could add your "voice" to those of the women represented here, what would you want to share with them? Why?

Resources

This section offers three different outlines for use in developing your own workshop, symposium, or conference, as well as some resources to assist you in your planning and discussion.

The first workshop outline, which utilizes a two-day format, and the second, which is based on a one-day format are for sample purposes only. Do not feel that they must be followed minute by minute. Make them your own; adapt them to reflect individual settings, needs, and objectives. The third outline covers a four-week period and takes the form of an adult education series. Again, the topics offered here are only suggestions. The design and purpose of such a series should encompass and address issues that are of concern to your local community.

Other resources to be found in this section are a membership roster of the NCCB Committee on Women in Society and in the Church; a selected bibliography; and additional resource references.

Sample Outline for Two-Day Workshop

Topic: Women in the Church and in Society

First Day: Women in the Church

9:00 - 9:30 a.m.	Registration
9:30 - 9:45 a.m.	Opening Prayer Service
10:00 - 11:30 a.m.	Keynote Address [Questions and answers follow.]
11:45 a.m. - 1:00 p.m.	Small-Group Discussions Group 1: Women's Spirituality Group 2: Women as Partners with Men in Ministry Group 3: Women in Canon Law
1:00 - 2:30 p.m.	Lunch [No speaker; participants should get acquainted with each other at tables seating no more than eight to twelve persons.]
2:30 - 4:30 p.m.	Panel: Women's Roles in the Parish/Diocesan Church [Presentation followed by questions and answers.]
4:30 - 5:00 p.m.	Free Time
5:00 - 6:00 p.m.	Liturgy
6:00 - 6:30 p.m.	Social Time
6:30 - 8:30 p.m.	Dinner [with speaker]

Second Day: Women in Society

9:00 - 9:15 a.m.	Morning Prayer
9:15 - 9:30 a.m.	Continental Breakfast
9:30 - 11:00 a.m.	Plenary Session [Questions and answers follow.]

11:15 a.m. - 12:15 p.m.	Small-Group Discussions
	   Group 1: Women as Immigrants: Are We Welcoming?
	   Group 2: Women as Care-givers
	   Group 3: Pro-Life as a True Feminist Position

12:30 - 1:45 p.m.	Lunch [No speaker; table seating same as day one.]
1:45 - 2:45 p.m.	Panel: Women's Roles and Standing in Society Today
2:45 - 4:30 p.m.	Wrap-Up and Open-Mike Session
4:45 - 5:00 p.m.	Closing Prayer Service

Sample Outline for One-Day Workshop

Topic

The theme should reflect a pressing issue/concern of women in your local area, for example: assistance for working mothers, including expanded daycare for children; fitting spirituality into the hectic life-style of women today as they fulfill roles of wife, mother, career woman, community activist, and so forth.

9:00 - 9:30 a.m.	Registration
9:30 - 9:45 a.m.	Morning Prayer Service [A prayer could be composed that reflects the theme selected for the workshop.]
10:00 - 11:00 a.m.	Keynote Address [The speaker should address the day's theme and set the tone for the workshop.]
11:15 a.m. - 12:15 p.m.	Small-Group Discussions [Discussions should focus on five points raised by the keynote address and reflect how the theme affects the participants.]
12:30 - 1:45 p.m.	Lunch
1:45 - 2:15 p.m.	Meditation Break [This should be a period of quiet for reflection on day's events so far. Encourage participants to visit a chapel if available, walk outside, or just sit quietly in the conference room.]

2:30 - 3:30 p.m.	Focus Groups	

[These groups should address the theme from a national viewpoint, indicating resources that are available from the Church at both the national and diocesan levels.]

3:45 - 5:00 p.m. General Session

[Share reports from the small-group discussions, including individual comments, so that all the participants feel that they are a part of the process.]

5:00 - 5:15 p.m. Wrap-Up

[The convener brings the workshop to a close. Inform the participants of the resources that are available from the NCCB Secretariat for Laity and Family Life, which will serve as facilitator for any follow-up.]

5:15 - 5:30 p.m. Evening Prayer Service

[This brief service could include the "Magnificat" and "Hail Mary."]

Sample Outline for Four-Part Adult Education Series

How to Proceed

- The series will include four sessions over a four-week period, perhaps during the season of Lent or Advent.

- Each session will begin and end promptly at the appointed times. They should last no more than two or two and one-half hours.

- Each session should have a leader to keep discussion focused and to make certain that each person has an opportunity to contribute. In addition, the leader should explain any ground rules to participants, for example:

    — No one should talk longer than five minutes at one time.

    — Each person should be listened to with respect.

    — Discussion should focus on the theme and on how it is pertinent to each person's life and interests.

- Distribute selected topical materials to participants, which should be read in advance of each meeting. Make certain they are neither too difficult nor too lengthy. Some advance work often makes for a livelier and more informed discussion.

Topics for Each Session

Week One: *Conversion*

— What is conversion?

— Why is it needed today to understand women and their concerns?

Resource: *The Wisdom of Women: Models for Faith and Action.* This book contains three presentations on the topic of conversion. Select one for use in this session.

Week Two: Women's Spirituality

— What nourishes women's prayer lives in your community?

— Who are the mystics of the Church who speak most directly to today's women?

— How is Mary a model for women?

Resources: Dana Greene's biography of *Evelyn Underhill: Artist of the Infinite Life* (New York: Crossroads, 1990), along with Underhill's own book, *Mysticism* (New York: New American Library, 1955).

Week Three: Women's Roles in Society and in the Church

— What are some of the roles being filled by women today in your local area (church, neighborhood, community)?

— What are some of the contributions women make to your local area?

— How many of these roles and contributions go largely unnoticed and unacknowledged?

— What are some simple ways to recognize the women who are making a difference in the life of your community?

Resources: *Listening to the Voices of Women.* 28-minute videotape. Available from: CTNA, 3211 Fourth Street, N.E., Washington, D.C. 20017-1194. Also four 10-minute videotapes, with study guides, on various aspects of women's lives: (1) *The Juggling Act: Women, Work, and Family;* (2) *Spirituality of Women;* (3) *Women and Men: Partners in Ministry;* and (4) *Mentoring.* Initial videotape in the series will be available beginning in September 1991, with staggered release dates for other series' entries continuing into 1992. Order from the USCC Office for Publishing and Promotion Services, 3211 Fourth Street, N.E., Washington, D.C. 20017-1194.

Week Four: Supporting Women Today

- Where and how do women find support for their needs today?

- What groups exist in your local parish/diocese to assist women (e.g., prayer groups, parenting groups, marriage enrichment)?

- What else could the local Church do to assist women today?

Resource: *GIFTS.* Quarterly publication of the NCCB Secretariat for Family, Laity, Women, and Youth features many articles by and about Catholic women. $6.00 annual subscription. Available from Secretariat for Family, Laity, Women, and Youth, 3211 Fourth Street, N.E., Washington, D.C. 20017-1194.

Membership Roster
Bishops' Committee on Women in Society and in the Church (1989-1992)

Chairman

Most Rev. Matthew H. Clark
Bishop of Rochester
1150 Buffalo Road
Rochester, New York 14624
Tel. 716-328-3210

Members

Most Rev. Thomas J. Murphy
Coadjutor Archbishop of Seattle
910 Marion Street
Seattle, Washington 98104
Tel. 206-382-4375

Most Rev. John R. Roach
Archbishop of St. Paul—
Minneapolis
226 Summit Avenue
St. Paul, Minnesota 55102
Tel. 612-291-4400

Most Rev. David Fellhauer
Bishop of Victoria
P.O. Box 4708
Victoria, Texas 77903
Tel. 512-573-0828

Most Rev. Joseph A. Francis, SVD
Auxiliary Bishop of Newark
139 Glenwood Avenue
East Orange, New Jersey 07017
Tel. 201-675-1997

Most Rev. Joseph L. Imesch
Bishop of Joliet
425 Summit Street
Joliet, Illinois 60435
Tel. 815-722-6606

Most Rev. Ricardo Ramirez
Bishop of Las Cruces
P.O. Box 16318
Las Cruces, New Mexico 88004
Tel. 505-523-7577

Most Rev. John J. Snyder
Bishop of St. Augustine
Catholic Center
P.O. Box 24000
Jacksonville, Florida 32241
Tel. 904-262-3200

Selected Bibliography

Aggeler, Maureen, RSCJ. *Mind Your Metaphors: A Critique of Language in the Bishops' Pastoral Letter on the Role of Women.* Mahwah, N.J.: Paulist Press, 1991.

Baker, Derek, ed. *Medieval Women.* Oxford, England: Basil Blackwell, 1979.

Carmody, Denise. *Feminism and Christianity: A Two-Way Reflection.* Washington, D.C.: University Press of America, 1990.

Carr, Anne E. *Transforming Grace.* New York: Harper Collins, 1990.

Coon, Linda L. *That Gentle Strength: Historical Perspectives on Women in Christianity.* Charlottesville, Va.: University Press of Virginia, 1990.

Dolan, Jay. *Transforming Parish Ministry: The Changing Role of Catholic Clergy, Laity and Women Religious.* New York: Crossroad Publishers, 1990.

Elizondo, Virgilio, ed. "Women in a Man's Church?" in *Concillium* 134. Edinburgh, Scotland: T. & T. Clark, n.d.

Frankiel, Tamar. *The Voice of Sarah: Feminine Spirituality and Traditional Judaism.* New York: Harper, 1990.

Giles, Mary. *The Feminist Mystic and Other Essays on Women and Spirituality.* New York: Crossroad Publishers, 1982.

Graham, Maureen. *Women of Power and Presence: The Spiritual Formation of Four Quaker Women Ministers.* Pendle Hill, Pa.: Pendle Hill Publishers, 1990.

Grana, Janice. *Images: Women in Transition.* Winona, Minn.: St. Mary's Press, 1977.

Grey, Mary. *Feminism, Redemption and the Christian Tradition.* Mystic, Conn.: Twenty-Third Publications, 1990.

Madeleva Lectures on Women's Spirituality. A variety of aspects on the topic, from women as prayers to women's creativity. Mahwah, N.J.: Paulist Press, n.d.

Mother Teresa. Part of the *People Who Have Helped the World* series. Wilton, Conn.: Morehouse Publishers, 1990.

National Conference of Catholic Bishops. "One in Christ Jesus: A Pastoral Response to the Concerns of Women for Church and Society," *Origins* 19:44. Washington, D.C.: Catholic News Service, 1990.

Newman, John. *Blessed Art Thou among Women.* Rockaway, N.J.: Dimension Books, 1985.

Pelikan, Jaroslav. *Eternal Feminine: Three Theological Allegories in Dante's "Paradiso."* Rutgers, N.J.: Rutgers University Press, 1990.

Rabuzzi, Kathryn A. *The Sacred and the Feminine: Toward a Theology of Housework.* New York: Harper, 1982.

Reilly, Maria, OP. *Wisdom Seeks Her Way: Liberating the Power of Women's Spirituality.* Washington, D.C.: Center of Concern, 1987.

Reilly, Maria OP, and Nancy Sylvester, IHM. *Trouble and Beauty: Feminist Meets Catholic Social Teaching.* Washington, D.C.: Center of Concern, 1991.

Sewell, Marilyn, ed. *Cries of the Spirit: Celebration of Women's Spirituality.* Boston, Mass.: Beacon Press, 1991.

Sleevi, Mary Lou. *Women of the Word.* Notre Dame, Ind.: Ave Maria Press, n.d.

Stendahl, Krister. *The Bible and the Role of Women: A Case Study in Hermeneutics.* Minneapolis, Minn.: Augsburg Fortress, 1966.

Wallace, Joanne. *The Working Woman.* Melbourne, Fla.: Dove Christian Books, 1986.

Willard, Frances. *Woman and Temperance; or, the Work and Workers of the Woman's Christian Temperance Union.* Salem, N.H.: Ayer Co., 1972.

Additional Resources

Diocesan Commissions on Women: What, Why, How—A Handbook. Available in September 1991 from the Secretariat for Family, Laity, Women, and Youth, National Conference of Catholic Bishops, 3211 Fourth Street N.E., Washington, D.C. 20017-1194.

GIFTS. A quarterly publication of the Secretariat for Family, Laity, Women, and Youth. Features many articles by and about Catholic women. $6.00 annual subscription. Available from Secretariat for Laity and Family Life, National Conference of Catholic Bishops, 3211 Fourth Street, N.E., Washington, D.C. 20017-1194.

Listening to the Voices of Women. 28-minute videotape. Order from CTNA, 3211 Fourth Street N.E., Washington, D.C. 20017-1194.

Videotape Series on Various Aspects of Women's Lives. Four 10-minute videotapes, with study guides: (1) *The Juggling Act: Women, Work, and Family;* (2) *Spirituality of Women;* (3) *Women and Men: Partners in Ministry;* and (4) *Mentoring.* Initial video in series available beginning in September 1991, with staggered release dates for other entries in series continuing into 1992. Order from the USCC Office for Publishing and Promotion Services, 3211 Fourth Street, N.E., Washington, D.C. 20017-1194.

The Wisdom of Women Symposium Poster. Available from Secretariat for Family, Laity, Women, and Youth, National Conference of Catholic Bishops, 3211 Fourth Street N.E., Washington D.C. 20017-1194.